Alpheus Felch

TO

Marie E. Zakrzewska, M. D.,

THIS VOLUME

IS CORDIALLY INSCRIBED

BY HER FRIEND,

THE TRANSLATOR.

MARIE DE ROHAN

CONNETABLE DE LUYNES DUCHESSE DE CHEVREUSE.

Engraved by Capewell & Kimmel from the Original Portrait

DELISSER & PROCTOR.

SECRET HISTORY

OF THE

FRENCH COURT

UNDER

RICHELIEU AND MAZARIN;

OR,

Life and Times of Madame de Chevreuse.

BY

VICTOR COUSIN,

AUTHOR OF "THE TRUE, THE BEAUTIFUL, AND THE GOOD," "COURSE OF PHILOSOPHY," "YOUTH OF MADAME DE LONGUEVILLE," ETC., ETC.

TRANSLATED BY

MARY L. BOOTH.

NEW YORK:

DELISSER & PROCTER, 508 BROADWAY,

(SUCCESSORS TO STANFORD & SWORDS.)

1859.

PREFACE BY THE TRANSLATOR.

Among the most admired of Victor Cousin's works are his "Studies of the Illustrious Women and the Society of the Seventeenth Century;" and of these none has excited so much attention as his "Life of Madame de Chevreuse." In this charming biography, which certainly reads very much like a romance, the author claims the merit of a scrupulous and exact adherence to the truth of history. He controverts many received opinions and forces the reader to abandon many established hypotheses, but he does it upon the incontestable evidence of cotemporary writers and of documents that were supposed to be lost or not known to exist. Among these are a hitherto unknown memoir of Richelieu concerning the secret affairs of 1633, which produced the imprisonment of Châteauneuf, keeper of the seals; the unpublished examinations of La Porte and the Abbess of Val-de-Grâce in 1637; the autograph *Carnets* of Mazarin, explained and developed by the evidence of his secret police, and several inedited letters of Queen Anne to the cardinal which solve the question of their relations.

Madame Chevreuse coped with Richelieu in the adroit political intrigues which marked the close of the reign of Louis XIII. and excited the admiration of all Europe; and in Cardinal Mazarin's memorable struggle at the beginning of his ministry and of the regency against the "Importants" (those predecessors of the "Frondeurs"), he encountered no more powerful adversary or none who gave him more anxiety than she. The author in his romantic memoir only rapidly sketches the early and the later life of his subject, dwelling most upon her career as an actress in the great drama of 1643; and his work was intended to be not so much the story of one of the most brilliant female politicians that France has ever produced, as a revelation of the secret history of the French Court under Richelieu and Mazarin.

CONTENTS.

FIRST PART.

MADAME DE CHEVREUSE AND RICHELIEU.

CHAPTER I.

CHAPTER II.

SECOND PART.

MADAME DE CHEVREUSE AND MAZARIN.

CHAPTER III.

CHAPTER IV.

MADAME DE CHEVREUSE;

OR,

SECRET HISTORY OF THE FRENCH COURT UNDER RICHELIEU AND MAZARIN.

Madame de Chevreuse and Richelieu.

CHAPTER I.

1600–1637.

Character and personal appearance of Madame de Chevreuse—Her birth and her first and second marriages—Intimate friendship with Anne of Austria—Count Holland—Prince de Chalais—First Exile—Charles IV. Duke of Lorraine—Return to France—Richelieu and Châteauneuf—Madame de Chevreuse banished again to Touraine—Affairs of 1637—Second Exile; flight to Spain.

If our readers are not wearied with our portraits of the women of the seventeenth century, we should be glad to present to them two new figures equally, though differently remarkable—two persons whom the caprice of Fate cast in the same age, the same party, amidst the same events, but who far from resembling each other, expressed, as we may say, the two opposite sides of the character, and the destiny of woman—both endowed with resplendent beauty, marvellous talent, and indomitable courage; yet the one as pure as beautiful, uniting in herself grace and dignity, everywhere inspiring love and commanding respect, at one time the idol and the favorite of a king without even the shadow of an injurious suspicion daring to raise itself against her, proud, even to haughtiness, towards the prosperous and powerful, gentle and compassionate to the oppressed and miserable, loving greatness, placing naught but virtue above position, mingling together the sparkling wit of a *precieuse*, the fastidiousness of a fashionable beauty, the intrepidity of a heroine, the dignity of a high-born lady, above all a Christian without bigotry, yet devout, and even austere, leaving behind her an odor of sanctity;[1] the other, perhaps more fascinating, of an irresistible grace and vivacity, full of talent, yet very ignorant, sharing in all the perils of the Catholic party, but scarcely thinking of religion, too proud to condescend to prudence, and curbed only by honor, devoted to gallantry, and counting all else as nothing, despising for the one whom she loved, danger, opinion and fortune, more restless than ambitious, and willingly staking her own life, as well as that of others; and after having passed her youth in intrigues of every sort, thwarting more than one plot, leaving on her path more than one victim, travelling over Europe as an exile, yet a conqueror, turning the heads of kings,—after having seen Chalais mount the scaffold, Châteauneuf expelled from the ministry, the Duke of Lorraine almost despoiled of his estates, Buckingham assassinated, the King of Spain engaged in an unsuccessful war, Queen Anne humiliated and vanquished, and Richelieu triumphant; sustaining the struggle to the end, always ready in this game of politics which had become her necessity and her passion, to descend to the darkest intrigues, and to make the rashest resolves; of an incomparable eye for recognizing the true position of affairs, and the enemy of the moment, and of a mind strong enough, and a heart bold enough to undertake to destroy him at any cost; a devoted friend, an implacable enemy almost without knowing hatred, in short, the most redoubtable

---

[1] The author alludes here to his life of Madame de Hautefort, which followed that of Madame de Chevreuse. Each biography, however, is complete in itself; this being the only allusion in the present volume to the subsequent memoir of Madame de Hautefort.—*Translator's Note.*

enemy encountered in turn by Richelieu and by Mazarin. The reader will easily divine that we speak of Madame de Hautefort and of Madame de Chevreuse.

Need we add that we do not intend to trace here fancy portraits, and that if we sometimes seem to recount romantic adventures, it is in conformity with all the rigor of the laws of history. These sketches, though fanciful in appearance, are worthy of the fullest confidence, and will soon be acknowledged as resting upon the testimony of approved cotemporary witnesses, or upon authentic documents as reliable as new, which will bear the scrutiny of the most exacting critic.

We commence with Madame de Chevreuse. She dates further back in the seventeenth century than does Madame de Hautefort—she at least precedes if she does not excel her. It must also be said that she filled a more lofty station, and played a more conspicuous part, and that her name belongs as much to the history of the politics as of the society of her age.

Madame de Chevreuse in truth[1] possessed almost all the qualities of a great politician, a single one was wanting, and it was the one precisely without which all the others ran to waste—she did not know how to propose to herself a just aim, or rather she never chose one for herself; it was another that chose for her. Madame de Chevreuse was a woman in the fullest sense—in this was her strength, and also her weakness. Her first impulse was love, or rather gallantry, and the interests of the one whom she loved became her chief aim. Here lies the solution of the prodigies of sagacity, adroitness and energy which she displayed in vain in the pursuit of a chimera, which

[1] Madame de Motteville, vol. i., Amsterdam edition of 1750, page 198:—"I heard her say to herself one day when I was complimenting her on having taken part in all the great events of Europe, that ambition had never touched her heart, but that affection had guided it, that is, that she had interested herself in the affairs of the world solely through sympathy with those whom she had loved." The passages of Retz, which we shall quote presently, may be reduced to the same interpretation.

constantly receded from her grasp, while it seemed to lure her on by the very prestige of difficulty and danger. Rochefoucauld accuses her of having brought misfortune on all whom she loved;[1] it is also just to say that all who loved her precipitated her in turn into their own mad enterprises. It was not she, apparently, who made of Buckingham a sort of Paladin without genius, of Charles IV. a brilliant adventurer, of Chalais a madman insane enough to pledge himself against Richelieu on the faith of the Duke of Orleans, and of Châteauneuf a restless second-rate aspirant, without being capable of attaining to be first. One must not believe that he knows Madame de Chevreuse when he has read the celebrated portrait which Retz has drawn of her, for this is exaggerated and overdrawn like all those of Retz, and was designed solely to gratify the malignant curiosity of Madame de Caumartin—without being really false, it is severe almost to injustice. Did it belong, indeed, to the restless and intemperate accomplice to become the pitiless censor of a woman in whose errors he had shared? Was he not also as much deceived as she, and for a much longer time? Did he show in the combat more address and courage, and in the defeat, more intrepidity and constancy? But Madame de Chevreuse has written us no memoirs in the easy and piquant style in which she retrieved her fortunes at the expense of the world. For our own part, we recognize two judges of her whose testimony cannot be regarded with suspicion—Richelieu and Mazarin. Richelieu did his best to gain her, and failing to succeed, treated her as an enemy worthy of himself; he exiled her repeatedly, and even after his death, when the gates of France were opened to all the outlaws, his implacable resentment—surviving him in the mind of the dying Louis XIII., closed them still upon her Read the *carnets* (note-books) and the confidential letters of

---

[1] Memoirs of Madame de Motteville, Coll. Petitot, second series, vol. ii., p. 339.

Mazarin attentively, and you will detect there the deep and continual anxiety which she caused him in 1643. Later, during the Fronde, he is found to be reconciled to her, and following her counsels, as judicious as they are bold. Finally, in 1660, when Mazarin, victorious everywhere, adds the treaty of the Pyrenees to that of Westphalia, and when Don Luis de Haro congratulates him on the repose which he is about to taste after so many storms, the cardinal replies, that one never can promise himself repose in France, and that even the women there are greatly to be feared. "You Spaniards may well speak of your ease," said he; "your women trouble themselves about nothing but love; but it is not so in France; we have three there now who would be quite capable of governing or of overthrowing three great kingdoms—the Duchess de Longueville, the Princess Palatine and Madame de Chevreuse."[1]

But first a word of the beauty of Madame de Chevreuse, for this beauty had a great share in her destiny. All her cotemporaries unite in celebrating it. A portrait nearly of life-size, which is in the possession of the Duke de Luynes, and which he has courteously shown to us,[2] gives her an enchanting figure, a charming face, large blue eyes, fine and luxuriant chestnut-hair, a beautiful bust, and a piquant mingling of refinement and vivacity, grace and passion in her whole person. This indeed was the character of the beauty of Madame de Chevreuse; we find it again in the excellent engraving of Daret,[3] which Harding has republished in England,

---

[1] *Vie de Madame de Longueville*, by Villefore, edition of 1739, second part, p. 33. Madame de Motteville, vol. i., *Ibid*:—"I have heard him say to those who were well acquainted with him, that no one had ever understood the interests of princes so well, or talked so well about them, and I have even heard him praise her capacity."

[2] This portrait is not an original, but a very ancient copy.

[3] See the collection in quarto of Daret, dedicated to Madame de Chevreuse herself. There is another engraved portrait of Madame de Chevreuse, which is very rare, in the collection of Leblond, in folio.

and also in the picture of Ferdinand Elle,[1] which represents her as a widow and aged. We feel in this last portrait that her dazzling beauty has passed away, but that acuteness, dignity, vivacity and grace are still surviving.

Marie de Rohan belonged to that ancient and illustrious family, the issue of the first sovereigns of Brittany, which, with its different branches, without counting its alliances, spread itself over, and long possessed, a considerable part of Brittany, dividing itself almost equally between the Catholic and the Protestant party in the sixteenth, and the commencement of the seventeenth centuries, zealously obeying royalty, and holding it in check by turns, and whose hereditary traits, strongly marked in both sexes, were loftiness of soul, bravery, and constancy. At the siege of Rochelle, two women, after enduring all the rigors of famine with the meanest of the soldiers, and subsisting like them upon horseflesh, chose rather to remain as prisoners in the hands of the enemy than to sign the articles of capitulation. These were the mother and the sister of the celebrated Duke de Rohan, one of our greatest warriors before Condé, and unquestionably our greatest military writer before Napoleon. The wife of this same Henri de Rohan defended Castres against the Marshal de Thémines. During the lapse of centuries, this noble house has not ceased to produce heroines of a resolute spirit, as well as beauties more brilliant than severe. In this respect, she whose history we are about to trace, showed no degeneracy from her race, she was truly of the blood of the Rohans.

She was daughter of Hercules de Rohan, Duke de Mont-

She is younger than in that of Daret, with an oval countenance, large eyes, a fine bust, and with hair curled and craped in the style of the beginning of the reign of Louis XIII. As to the ugly little portraits of Moncornet, they have no resemblance to Madame de Chevreuse at any age.

[1] The original of Ferdinand Elle is at the house of the Duke de Luynes. Balechou has engraved it for *L'Europe Illustre.*

bazon, a zealous servant of Henri IV., Peer and Master of the Hounds, and Governor of Paris and of the Isle of France, and of his first wife, Madeleine de Lenoncourt, sister of Urbain de Laval, Marshal de Bois-Dauphin. Born almost with the seventeenth century, in December, 1600, she lost her mother at a very early age, and in 1617 espoused that audacious favorite of Louis XIII., who, on the faith of the fickle friendship of a king, dared attempt to overthrow the authority of the queen-mother, Marie de Medicis, destroyed the Marshal d'Ancre, combated the Princes and the Protestants at the same time, and attempted against Richelieu himself the system of Richelieu. Let us ask in passing, Is it not unworthy of history to attribute the elevation of Luynes to the caprice of a king, who takes one of his pages, a petty gentleman, for his prime minister, solely because he finds him skilful in the art of training falcons? Such, perhaps, was the beginning of the fortunes of Luynes,—such was not the cause of it. This petty gentleman, son of *Captain de Luynes*, as he was called, one of the bravest and most intelligent of the officers of Henri IV., was himself a man of talent and courage, who, under the direct inspiration of Louis XIII., honorably restored and sustained while he lived the work of the great king which Richelieu had at first opposed in his character of the favorite of Marie de Medicis, and which he afterwards undertook with great zeal, gradually turning against his old friends and his first protectress, so far as to exile her precisely as De Luynes had done.[1] The young

---

[1] The reader should not be duped by the memoirs of Richelieu, which are designed, like all memoirs, to deceive posterity in favor of the author. Richelieu did not begin his career as he finished it. He commenced as a partisan of the Spanish Alliance to please the queen-mother. There is a production of Richelieu, now very rare, entitled, *Harangue prononcée en la salle du Petit Bourbon, le 23 fevrier*, 1615, *a la clôture des états tenus a Pàris, par révérend père en Dieu, messire Armand Jean du Plessis de Richelieu, évesque de Luçon.* In this, Richelieu congratulates the king, who was of age, on having "restored the reins of this great em-

and ambitious constable was well fitted to please the bold heart of the beautiful Marie, and she loved him faithfully. She had one daughter, a devotee, who died unmarried, and a son who played a *rôle* in the seventeenth century by his *liaisons* at Port Royal, translated into French the Meditations of Descartes, wrote estimable works of piety, under the name of M. de Laval, and continued the illustrious house.

The Duchess and Constabless de Luynes, left a widow in 1621, in 1622 espoused in a second marriage Claude de Lorraine, Duke de Chevreuse, one of the sons of Henri de Guise, Grand Chamberlain of France. His greatest merit lay in his name, and the good looks and valor which could never be wanting in a prince of the house of Lorraine; but he was disorderly in his business, and disagreeable in his manners, which may explain and extenuate the faults of his wife. Three daughters were born of this new marriage, two of whom died

---

pire to the hands of the queen, his mother, so that she might have for some time the guidance of his estates." Spain and France "being united, have nothing to fear; while separated, they can only receive injury from each other." Let us add that Luynes, struck with the talents of Richelieu, ended by extricating him from disgrace; that he proposed to restore him to public life, and, to attach him to himself, caused the niece of Richelieu, Mademoiselle du Pont de Courlay, afterwards Duchess de Aiguillon, to espouse his own nephew, Combalet. Richelieu therefore was at that time regarded as serving Luynes in an underhand way, and it is principally to efface and contradict this well-founded rumor, that, uniting all the foibles and weaknesses of vanity to the aspirations and ambition of pride, he attempts in his memoirs to decry the constable, reproaching him with that of which he himself was afterwards guilty. Luynes resolutely attacked and promptly subdued the rebellious princes, and by means of the treaty of Angoulême secured the queen-mother in a necessary exile without useless rigor. When Rohan and Soubise dared to draw the sword, the new Duke de Luynes gained the title of constable by opposing the Protestants, and he undertook the siege of Montauban, the precursor of that of La Rochelle. In 1620, Bearn was definitively incorporated with the crown. This is an abstract of the whole of Richelieu's career.

in convents,[1] the third was the beautiful and celebrated Mademoiselle de Chevreuse, who was weak enough to listen to Retz, if we may believe his assertions, for which he repaid her by caricaturing her for the diversion of the one for whom he wrote.[2]

The new Duchess de Chevreuse had been appointed superintendent of the queen's household during the life-time of her first husband, and had soon become the favorite of Anne of Austria as the constable was the favorite of Louis XIII. The court at that time was very brilliant, and gallantry the order of the day. Marie de Rohan was naturally gay and spirited. She yielded to the allurements of youth and pleasure. She had lovers, and these lovers forced her into politics. Retz himself admits this in the following passage, too famous to be omitted here, though we must first remark that even if it have a groundwork of truth, the coloring is greatly exaggerated:[3] "I never saw any one else," he says, "in whom intuition could supply the place of judgment. She often suggested expedients so brilliant that they seemed like flashes of lightning, and so wise that they would not have been disowned by the greatest men of any age. Yet these were only called forth by the occasion. If she had lived in an age in which there were no politics, she never would have invented any. If the prior of the Carthusians had pleased her, she would have become a recluse in good faith. M. de Lorraine first forced her into public affairs,

[1] One, Anne Marie de Lorraine, died in 1652, aged eighteen, the Abbess of the Port aux Dames; the other, Henriette de Lorraine, was Abbess de Jouarre. The latter must not be confounded with her niece, Madame Albert de Luynes, who, with one of her sisters, was also a devotee at Jouarre, and to whom Bossuet wrote so many touching letters. Henriette de Lorraine had some disputes with her bishop respecting the extent of the power of abbesses, and, after yielding, she retired to Port Royal, where she died in 1694.—*Gallia Christiana*, vol. viii., p. 1715; *Vie de Bossuet*, by M. de Beausset, vol. ii. Book vii.

[2] Vol. i. of the Amsterdam edition, 1731, p. 221.

[3] *Ibid.*, p. 219.

the Duke of Buckingham and Count Holland sustained her in them, Châteauneuf interested her in them. She abandoned herself to them as she would unhesitatingly have abandoned herself to any thing that pleased the one whom she loved, without choice, and simply because it was necessary to her nature that she should love some one. She was easily persuaded to accept of any lover,[1] but when she had once taken him, she loved him truly and faithfully, and she has confessed to Madame de Rhodes and myself that, by a strange caprice, those whom she had most esteemed she had never loved, with the exception of the unhappy Buckingham. Her devotion to a passion which may be called eternal, however often she may have changed its object, did not prevent a patch upon her face from abstracting her attention,[2] but she always returned to her subject with a fascinating grace that made this little break absolutely enchanting. Never did person care less for perils, and never had woman more contempt for scruples and for duties,—she knew no duty but that of pleasing her lover." Of this sketch, which might have moved Tallemant to envy, retain at least these striking and faithful traits—the prompt and sure penetration of Madame de Chevreuse, her indomitable courage, and her loyalty and devotion in love. Besides, Retz is entirely mistaken as to the order of her adventures, he forgets some, and he invents others; he seems to regard the events in which the passions of Madame de Chevreuse caused her to take part as trifles, while in fact there were none greater or more tragical. Let us throw aside this trifling and frivolous style, and seek in its stead to establish the truth.

The young queen, Anne of Austria, and her youthful super-

---

[1] A ridiculous calumny, the sole pretext of which is he last *liaison* of Madame de Chevreuse during the Fronde. See our last chapter.

[2] This accusation simply means that "Madame de Chevreuse was subject to fits of abstraction during her conversation," as Madame de Motteville informs us. Vol. i., p. 198.

intendent, who were nearly of the same age, only occupied themselves at first with frivolous pastimes. Anne, neglected by her husband, consoled herself with the society and the lively and happy humor of Madame de Chevreuse. They passed their time together, making of every thing "food for their wit and pleasantry: *a giovine cuor tutto è giuoco.*" Lord Rich, afterwards the celebrated Count Holland, of the house of Warwick, came to the French court at the close of 1624, or the commencement of 1625, to demand the hand of the beautiful Henriette, sister of Louis XIII., for the Prince of Wales, who soon after became Charles I. During this negotiation, the Count became enamored with Madame de Chevreuse. He was young and singularly handsome; he pleased her, and won her over to the interests of England. This was, I believe, the true *debut* of Madame de Chevreuse, both in love and in politics. Holland, who was volatile, and a lover of pleasure and intrigue,[1] persuaded her to entangle her royal friend in some love affair like their own. Anne of Austria was vain and coquettish, she loved to please, and with her country's taste for gallantry, aided by the freedom in which she was left by Louis XIII., she did not interdict herself from accepting homage; but here the game was not without danger, and the handsome and elegant Buckingham succeeded in seriously troubling the heart of the queen. It was not the fault of Madame de Chevreuse if Anne of Austria did not wholly yield. Buckingham was rash and the superintendent complaisant; and the queen only escaped at a perilous risk.

Whatever Retz may say of it, we doubt very much whether Buckingham was ever any thing more to Madame de Chevreuse than the intimate friend of her lover, and the chief of the party into which Holland had drawn her. She saw him for the first

---

[1] La Rochefoucauld, ibid., p. 340; La Porte, *Memoires*, Coll. Petitot, 2d series, vol. lix., p. 295: "One of the handsomest men in the world, but of an effeminate beauty."

time in May, 1625, when he came to France to espouse Madame in behalf of Charles I., and, at that time, Buckingham was in the height of his infatuation for Queen Anne, while Madame de Chevreuse was in love with Count Holland, whom she soon rejoined in England, having had the art to cause herself to be appointed to escort the new Princess of Wales to her husband. Now, when Madame de Chevreuse loved, as Retz himself affirms, she loved faithfully and exclusively. At the age of twenty-four, one does not trifle with a first attachment to the extent of giving one's own lover to another, and the *rôle* which the poor woman already plays in this affair is not so honorable as to make us delight to vilify her still more. Madame de Chevreuse fell ill, it is true, on hearing the news of the assassination of Buckingham. Nothing was more natural; she lost in him a tried friend, the confidant of her first love, and the chief and the hope of the enemies of Richelieu. To the obscure insinuations of Retz, should be opposed the clear and connected account of La Rochefoucauld, and above all, the silence of Tallemant,[1] who would not have failed to add this item to his scandalous chronicles, had he ever heard the story. Thus, without pretending to scan such things clearly, especially after the lapse of two centuries, but following our rule of admitting nothing except from sure testimony, we incline to the belief that the Duke of Buckingham should be struck from the list, still very numerous, of the lovers of Madame de Chevreuse, and that the handsome Chalais was the immediate successor of the elegant Count Holland in the heart of the beautiful duchess.

Without making of the conspiracy of Chalais, as Richelieu would have it, "the most frightful conspiracy of which history has ever made mention,"[2] we cannot refuse to admit that it was not so trifling an affair as Chalais asserted, trembling for his

[1] Vol. i., p. 241.

[2] *Memoires* of Richelieu in the Coll. Petitot, vol. iii., p. 64.

head. The court of Monsieur was already a focus of intrigues against Richelieu. Monsieur did not like his proposed marriage with Mademoiselle de Montpensier, and Anne of Austria, on her side, who had as yet no children, feared a marriage which might some day take the crown from her head, and transfer it to the house of Orleans. Henri de Talleyrand, Prince de Chalais, of the house of Perigord, came to the aid of Monsieur and the queen; he planned some dark intrigue[1] which Richelieu, perhaps, exaggerated, but which he succeeded in so firmly establishing in the mind of the king, that Louis XIII. not only abandoned Chalais as afterwards he abandoned Cinq-Mars, but remained persuaded during his whole life that the queen had been implicated in the affair, and that, he being dead or dethroned, she and Monsieur had entertained the thought of a union. Chalais mounted the first scaffold erected by Richelieu, despite the tears of his aged mother. Monsieur

---

[1] La Rochefoucauld, ibid., p. 339: "Chalais was master of the wardrobe; his person and mind were attractive, and he was devotedly attached to Madame de Chevreuse. He was accused of having formed a design against the life of the king, and of having proposed to Monsieur to break off his marriage with a view of espousing the queen on his accession to the throne. Although this crime was not fully proved, Chalais was beheaded, and the cardinal had but little difficulty in persuading the king that the queen and Madame de Chevreuse had not been ignorant of the design of Chalais." Fontenay-Mareuil, *Memoires*, Coll. Petitot, vol. li., p. 23: "M. de Chalais was young, well formed, expert in all kinds of exercise, and above all, agreeable in society; which rendered him a great favorite among the women, who finally caused his ruin. Fontenay says that in the midst of the affair, and despite all his pledges, he became reconciled to Richelieu, but that Madame de Chevreuse reproached him so bitterly and urged him on so strongly, that, nothing being impossible to a woman of so much beauty and wit, he was unable to resist her, and chose rather to be unfaithful to the cardinal and himself than to her, so that he had no sooner caused Monsieur to change his opinion, than he rendered him again more rebellious than ever. Had he merely counselled Monsieur to leave the court to go to La Rochelle, no one could have saved him; but it is said, and many believed it, that he went much farther.

extricated himself from the affair by espousing Mademoiselle de Montpensier, the queen fell more deeply than ever into disgrace, and Madame de Chevreuse, perfidiously denounced by the Duke of Orleans, and also by Chalais himself, who, with his dying breath, vainly denied his first confessions, was condemned to depart from France. What part had she had in this conspiracy? That which both love and friendship had forced upon her. Chalais was her lover, and she was devoted to Anne of Austria. She was no more the originator of this plot than of any of the others which the Duke of Orleans so often commenced but never finished; but, on entering it, she brought into it all her ardor and her energy. Richelieu says, and we believe him, that "she did more harm than any one else." [1] She dearly learned the cost of loving a queen too well. Anne of Austria escaped with a slight humiliation, but her courageous confidant saw the man whom she loved perish by the hand of the executioner, and herself torn from all the refinements of life, from the fêtes of the Louvre and from her beautiful château of Dampierre, and forced to seek an asylum in a foreign land. "Then," says Richelieu, "she was transported with rage." She even went so far as to say that they did not know her; that they thought that she only had mind enough for coquetry, but she would show them in time that she was capable of something else; that there was nothing that she would not do to avenge herself; and that she would abandon herself to a soldier of the guards rather than not obtain satisfaction from her enemies. She wished to go to England, where she was sure of the support of Holland, of Buckingham, and of Charles I. himself. This favor was not accorded her; her imprisonment was even talked of, and it was with difficulty that her husband obtained permission for her to retire into Lorraine.

It is well known that, instead of a refuge, she found there

---

[1] *Memoires*, vol. iii., p. 105.

a most brilliant triumph. She dazzled, seduced and urged on the impetuous and adventurous Charles IV.[1] She was not, as La Rochefoucauld has said, and as others have so often repeated, the primary cause of the misfortunes of this prince;—no, the true cause of the misfortunes of Charles IV. lay in his own character—in his presumptuous ambition, open to every wild fancy, which had to encounter such a politician as Richelieu. Let us not forget that these two personages were embroiled long before Madame de Chevreuse set foot in Nancy. Richelieu claimed several portions of the estates of the duke, who, being placed between Austria and France, began the warfare by declaring in favor of the former against the latter. He was the man the best fitted of all others to share the sentiments of Madame de Chevreuse, as she was admirably suited to second his designs. She found Charles IV. already pledged to Austria, she attached him to England, then ruled by Buckingham; she also established intelligence with Savoy, and thus formed a European league by which she secured to the interior the support of the Protestant party, controlled by her relatives, Rohan and Soubise. The plan was well laid; an English fleet, commanded by Buckingham himself, would disembark at the Isle of Ré and join the Protestants of La Rochelle; the Duke of Savoy would make a descent at the same time upon Dauphiny and Provence; and the Duke de Rohan, at the head of the Reformers, would stir up Languedoc, while the Duke of Lorraine should march towards Paris by the way of Champagne. The principal agent of this plan, charged with bearing mes-

---

[1] Here, as well as in respect to the early part of the life of Madame de Chevreuse, we refer our readers to the work of Count d'Haussonville, *Histoire de la réunion de la Lorraine à la France*, with inedited notes, proofs and historical documents, of which excellent treatise we would give a more extended eulogy if competent critics had not anticipated us by diffusing the knowledge, wit and elegance which illuminate its pages.

sages to all the interested parties, was Lord Montagu, an intimate friend of Holland and of Buckingham, who, it is said, also suffered himself to be captivated by the charms of Madame de Chevreuse.

Richelieu, forewarned by his own sagacity, and by his police, watched all the movements of Montagu, dared to cause his arrest on the Lorraine territory,[1] seized his papers, discovered the whole conspiracy, and faced it with his accustomed vigor. The principal attack upon the Isle of Ré was foiled, and Buckingham forced to an ignominious retreat. La Rochelle soon after yielded to the perseverance

---

[1] Queen Anne was so deeply involved in this intrigue, that she trembled for her own safety when news of the arrest of Montagu reached her, and she could not rest until she was well assured that she was not named in the papers of the prisoner, and would not be mentioned in his examination. La Porte, *Memoires*, p. 304: "The news of the arrest of Lord Montagu threw the queen into the greatest anxiety. She feared that she was named in his papers, and that when this came to the ears of the king, with whom she did not live on very good terms, he would treat her harshly and send her to Spain, as he assuredly would have done. So great was her disquietude, that she neither ate nor slept. In this embarrassment she recollected that I was in a company of *gendarmes* which belonged to the troops appointed to attend Lord Montagu. She therefore inquired for me of Lavau, who found me and conducted me after midnight to the chamber of the queen, whence all had withdrawn. She told me of her anxiety, and that, having no person in whom she could confide, she had sought me, believing that I would serve her from affection and with fidelity, and that her safety or destruction depended on the news which I should bring to her. She told me the whole affair, and said that I must endeavor in my attendance on Lord Montagu, to speak to him and to learn whether she was named in the papers which had been taken, and whether, in the event of his being examined while in the Bastille, and urged to reveal the confederates of this league, he would refrain from naming her. . . . I related the trouble of the queen to Lord Montagu, who replied that she was neither directly nor indirectly named in the papers, and assured me that, if he were questioned, he would die rather than say aught that might injure her. La Porte says that when he brought back this answer to the queen, she danced for joy.

and skill of the cardinal, the vanquished coalition was dissolved, and England sued for peace, placing, among its most urgent conditions, the return of the beautiful exile, now become a political power for whom peace or war was made. "She was a princess who was much loved in England, and one for whom the king entertained an especial regard, and he would assuredly have insisted on including her in the treaty of peace if he had not been ashamed of making mention of a woman in it; but he would be greatly obliged if his majesty would not displease him in this. She had a fine mind, a potent beauty which she knew how to use to advantage, was never disheartened by any misfortune, and always retained her evenness of temper;"[1] a less brilliant, but far more just and faithful portrait than that of Retz, and which may have been drawn by Richelieu's own hand, as it is probable that the cardinal, according to his custom, has here recapitulated the propositions of Montagu in his own style, instead of copying them verbatim. Be this as it may, Richelieu, who ardently desired to disengage himself from the Rohans, the Protestants, and England, in order to direct all his forces against Spain, accepted the desired condition, and Madame de Chevreuse returned to Dampierre.

A few years of tranquillity followed this turbulent life. Marie de Rohan reappeared at court in all her beauty. She was not yet thirty years of age, and one could scarcely look at her with impunity. Richelieu himself was not insensible to her charms;[2] he endeavored to please her, but his homage was not accepted. To the all-powerful cardinal, Madame de Chevreuse preferred one of his ministers; and the one upon whom he had the best reason to count; she conquered him with a glance, and won him over to the party of the queen and the malcontents.

---

[1] *Memoires* of Richelieu, Vol. iv., p. 74.

[2] Madame de Motteville, Vol. i., p. 62: "This minister, despite the rigor with which he had treated her, had never disliked her; her beauty had charmed him etc."

Charles de l'Aubépine, Marquis de Châteauneuf, of an ancient family of counsellors and secretaries of state, had succeeded Michael Marillac in the office of Keeper of the Seals in 1630; this he owed to the favor of Richelieu, and to the attachment which he had shown him. He had carried this devotion very far, for he had presided at Toulouse over the commission which had sentenced the imprudent and unfortunate Montmorenci, and had thus drawn upon himself the eternal enmity of the Montmorencis and the Condés. Châteauneuf had therefore given bloody pledges of fidelity to Richelieu, and they seemed inseparable. The cardinal had loaded him with favors, as was his custom towards his friends. Châteauneuf had been appointed chancellor of the royal orders, and Governor of Touraine. He was a consummate man of business, laborious and active, and endowed with that quality which best pleased the cardinal, resolution; but he had an inordinate ambition which he retained through life, and which when joined with love, rendered him blind to all but his purpose.[1] We cannot but smile when we recall the assertion of

---

[1] Richelieu, *Testament Politique*, Chap. i.: "The important post to which your majesty had appointed him, the hundred thousand crowns which he received each year from your liberality, the government of one of your provinces, all extraordinary marks of favor to a man in his position, were not considerations weighty enough to deter him from becoming the author of his own ruin." *Memoires*, Vol. vii., p. 326: "M. de Châteauneuf was made Keeper of the Seals in the belief that he would be guided solely by the commandments of the king, and the interests of his service, as he had hitherto seemed to have no other design, and had been for many years attached to the cardinal, serving him with many tokens of affection and fidelity; but no sooner was he emancipated by the authority of his office and placed in an independent position, than the designs which before had been concealed by respect and fear, began to disclose themselves. He attached himself to the cabals of the court, particularly to that of factious women headed by the Duchess de Chevreuse, whose conduct had often displeased the king, inasmuch as she had not only belonged to all the troublesome factions that had been raised against him, but had formerly been herself the very dangerous leader of a party."

Retz, that Châteauneuf amused Madame Chevreuse with public affairs. This amusement must have been of a very peculiar nature indeed, since she staked in it her fortune, and sometimes her head, and the intrigue in which they both were engaged was so rash, that here, at least, it must be admitted that it was not Châteauneuf who forced Madame de Chevreuse into it, but rather she who urged on the keeper of the seals.

Châteauneuf was then fifty years of age,[1] and the sentiment that he had conceived for Madame de Chevreuse must have been one of those fatal passions which precede and mark the final departure of youth. As to Madame de Chevreuse, she shared to the fullest extent in the dangers and misfortunes of Châteauneuf, and never afterwards consented to separate his fortunes from her own. In all her aberrations, she at least preserved this remnant of honor, that when she loved, she loved with unbounded fidelity, and after the passion had passed away, she still maintained for its object an inviolable friendship. For some time, Richelieu had perceived that his keeper of the seals was no longer the same. His suspicious nature, seconded by his penetration and his incomparable police, had put him on the track of the most secret manœuvres of Châteauneuf, and he afterwards amused himself by collecting all the proofs of the treason of his former friend in papers which have hitherto remained unpublished, and which seem to us to be a stray chapter of his *Memoires.*[2] It is said that, during an illness which threatened the life of the cardinal, Anne of Austria gave a ball, at which Châteauneuf appeared

---

[1] He was born in 1580. An excellent crayon portrait of D. Demonstier, engraved by Ragot, represents him as keeper of the seals, with a firm and lofty bearing.

[2] We found this curious fragment in the archives of foreign affairs, FRANCE, vol. ci., being the last article of the volume, under the title: *Memoire de M. le Cardinal de Richelieu, contre M. de Châteauneuf*, consisting of twelve pages in the well-known handwriting of Charpentier, one of the secretaries of the cardinal.

and danced;[1] a signal act of folly which opened the eyes of Richelieu, and incensed him greatly. On the twenty-fifth of December, 1633, the keeper of the seals was arrested, and all his papers seized. Fifty-two letters in the handwriting of Madame de Chevreuse were found, in which, under an easily-read cypher and through a transparent disguise, the designs of Châteauneuf and the duchess were discovered. There were also many letters from the Chevalier de Jars, Count Holland, Montagu, Puylaurens, Count de Brion, the Duke de Vendôme, and even from the Queen of England. These papers were carried to the cardinal, who preserved them; after his death, they were found in his casket, and thus fell into the hands of the Marshal de Richelieu, who transmitted them to Père Griffet for his *Histoire du règne du Louis XIII.*[2] An ancient copy is now in the possession of the Duke de Luynes, whose spirit is too noble to seek to screen from history the well-known faults of his illustrious ancestress, especially since these faults bear the stamp of a noble heart and lofty character. We have carefully examined these curious manuscripts, particularly the letters of Madame de Chevreuse. They show that Richelieu was assiduously attentive to her, that he was jealous of M. de Châteauneuf,[3] and that the latter was alarmed by the circumspection which she preserved towards the prime minister, the better to conceal from him their intercourse and plans. We cannot read without interest different passages of these letters, in which we perceive the sprightly yet audacious wit of the duchess, her power over the

---

[1] *Memoires de Richelieu*, vol. vii., p. 148; Editor's Note.

[2] See this excellent but unappreciated work, vol. ii., p. 392.

[3] The jealousy of Richelieu towards Châteauneuf appears in the following extract from the *Memoires* of La Porte, ibid., p. 322: "The cardinal questioned me closely about the queen, whether M. de Châteauneuf went often to her palace, if he was late there, and whether he did not generally go to the chateau of Madame de Chevreuse."

keeper of the seals, and her fearless enmity to the cardinal, despite the deference with which she treated him.:—

"Madame de Chevreuse complains to M. de Châteauneuf of her servant, who has so little faith in the generosity and friendship of his master,[1] and who does very wrong when he asks whether Madame de Chevreuse neglects him to pledge herself to the cardinal. You do wrong to have this thought; the mind of Madame de Chevreuse is too noble for treacherous sentiments ever to enter it. This is why I regard the favor of the cardinal no more than his power, and I shall never do any thing unworthy of myself, either for the good which I may gain from the one, or the evil which I may suffer from the other. Believe this if you would do me justice. I shall devote my whole life to you; and remember that you have the advantage here, for I shall take great pleasure in pleasing you, and shall suffer much in displeasing you. These, conscientiously, are my sentiments, and you have no share in them if ever you displease your master.

"Madame de Chevreuse has seen the cardinal, who remained two hours at the palace of the queen. He paid her extravagant compliments, and uttered the most extraordinary flatteries in the presence of Madame de Chevreuse, to whom he spoke very coldly, affecting great negligence and indifference, while she treated him in her usual manner, without seeming to notice his mood. Upon his attempting to taunt her, Madame de Chevreuse jested at him in open defiance of his power. This surprised rather than irritated him, for he then changed his tone, and attempted courtesies and the greatest humility. I do not know whether he acted thus to conceal his ill-humor in the presence of the queen, or whether he did

---

[1] The reader will note that these letters are translated almost verbatim from the original, and that the frequent changes which occur in person and tense are designed to throw a veil—transparent enough, it is true—over the correspondence.—NOTE BY THE TRANSLATOR.

not wish to embroil himself with Madame de Chevreuse. I shall see him to-morrow at two o'clock. I will send you word of all that passes. Rest assured that Madame de Chevreuse will only live for the world while she lives for you."

"I believe that I am destined to be the object of the folly of madmen. The cardinal is a good proof of this; but whatever trouble his ill-humor may give me, it does not afflict me so much as does that of 37,[1] (probably Brion, or perhaps de Thou,) who, without listening to my entreaties, or to the reasons which I have given him, insists on visiting Madame de Chevreuse, and says that nothing shall prevent him, even though Madame de Chevreuse tells him that she does not wish it, for fear of offending the cardinal. Should he discover it, I confess to you that the language of 37 troubles me greatly, for I cannot suffer it. I am sorry that 37 should have given me so many causes of annoyance after having given me so many reasons to be pleased with him. I am resolved not to see him if he come against my wishes, and not to receive his letters if he does not repent of the manner in which he has addressed Madame de Chevreuse, who can suffer this language from none other than you."

"Madame de Chevreuse has had no news from the cardinal. If he is as satisfied with not hearing from me as I am with hearing no more from him, he is well pleased, and I am freed from that persecution from which may time and our good angel deliver us!

"The tyranny of the cardinal increases every moment. He storms and rages because Madame de Chevreuse does not go to see him. I have written to him twice with compliments of which he is unworthy, and which I should never have offered to him, had it not been for the persecution of M. de Chevreuse, who said that these would purchase my repose. I believe that

---

[1] In the original, Madame de Chevreuse is designated by number 28; Châteauneuf by 38; the cardinal by 22; Louis XIII. by 23; Queen Anne by 24; M. de Chevreuse by 57, etc.

the favors of the king have carried his presumption to its highest point. He fancies that he can terrify Madame de Chevreuse by his anger, and persuades himself, in my opinion, that she will leave nothing untried to appease it; but she is resolved to perish rather than to submit to the cardinal. His glory is odious to me. He has said to my husband that my caprices were insupportable to a man of his temper, and that he was resolved no longer to pay me any special attention, since I was incapable of giving my friendship and confidence to him alone. I tell you this in confidence. Feign not to know it to M. de Chevreuse. He has had a little quarrel with me, for he has been so intimidated by the insolence of the cardinal that he wishes to persecute me into a base endurance of him. I esteem your courage and affection so highly that I wish you to know all the interests of Madame de Chevreuse. She confides so entirely in you that she believes them to be as safe in your hands as in her own. Love your master faithfully, and however persecuted he may be, believe that in all his actions he will prove himself worthy of love.

"I shall make no excuses to-day for not having written to you, but I wish you to believe that I have not ceased to think of you, although my letters have not expressed it to you. I can only describe the interview between the cardinal and Madame de Chevreuse by saying that he showed as much passion for your master as Madame de Chevreuse formerly thought existed in the heart of 33;[1] but that Madame de Chevreuse always regarded as a true passion, whereas she believes this of the cardinal to be a feigned one. He told her that he had now no secrets from her, and that he would positively do all that she commanded him, provided that she would live in such a manner with him as to assure him that he stood higher in her esteem and confidence than any other on earth. . . . The one who promised to bring me news was here yesterday, but

[1] The Duke of Lorraine, or Count Holland.

was very much cast down; two or three times he seemed to wish to tell me something, and I gave him sufficient opportunity, but he remained silent, and I know nothing of his sentiments except what I surmise. As soon as I know the truth, you shall be informed of it, and I will avail myself of it with him and with all the rest as I have promised you; be sure of this, and also that the promises of the cardinal will not shake me. Need I assure you of this? Can it be possible that you would even suspect it? I should be in despair if I believed so, but I have too good an opinion of you not to live in the certainty that you have not a bad one of me.

"I am driven to despair by what the cardinal has demanded of Madame de Chevreuse this evening. He has despatched a messenger to her to entreat of her two things: first, that she would not speak to Brion, (François Christophe de Levis, Count de Brion, one of the favorites of the Duke of Orleans, the future Duke de Damville,) and second, that she would not see M. de Châteauneuf. It is only the last that troubles me. However, my resolution of testifying my affection to M. de Châteauneuf is stronger than all considerations of the cardinal. I have therefore sent word to the cardinal that I cannot refuse the entreaties of M. de Chevreuse that I should see M. de Châteauneuf respecting several of his business affairs. My own chief business is to acquit myself of the obligations which I owe to M. de Châteauneuf, to whom I am more indebted than to any other person.

"There is no pleasure or fatigue which can prevent me from thinking of you, and from giving you tokens of it. These three lines are a proof of this truth, and I wish them to serve as the assurance of another, namely, that if M. de Châteauneuf is as devoted a servant in deeds as in words, Madame de Chevreuse will be a more grateful master in actions than in language.

"I do not doubt the trouble which you are in, and you protest that Madame de Chevreuse shares it, believing her the cause. Send me word how I can see you without the knowledge of the cardinal; for I will do any thing you may deem proper for this, wishing ardently to converse with you, and having many things to say to you which cannot well be explained in writing, especially concerning 37[1] and the cardinal, but the latter more particularly, having seen him this evening, and found him more than ever resolved to persecute Madame de Chevreuse. He parted on good terms with her, but she never found him in such a mood as to-day; so restless and so variable in his manner, now carried away by anger, then pacified in a moment into extreme humility. He cannot endure that Madame de Chevreuse should esteem M. de Châteauneuf, but he cannot prevent her; this I promise you, my faithful servant, whom I so call, because I believe him to be such. Adieu, I must see you at any cost. Send me an answer, and beware of the cardinal, who watches Madame de Chevreuse and M. de Châteauneuf, in whom Madame de Chevreuse confides as in herself.

"I would truly have given my life to have seen you yesterday. I went out in the evening, and was near going for this purpose to your sister's house, (Elisabeth de L'Aubéspine, who had married André de Cochefilet, Count de Vaucellas.) If the cardinal speaks to you of the visit of Madame de Chevreuse, tell him that it was respecting the affair of the Princess de Guymené, (sister-in-law of Madame de Chevreuse;) but I wish you to seem to be displeased with your master, and to despise him. I know that this will be painful to you, nevertheless you must obey me, because it is absolutely necessary. It is for this reason that I recommend it to you. Choose a favorable occasion for this. Do not send to my house. You shall often have news from me, and during my whole life, proofs of my affection. I shall be to-day where you are going.

"Although I am ill, I will not refrain from telling you the

[1] See a preceding reference to 37.

result of the visit of Madame de Chevreuse to the cardinal. He spoke of his passion, which, he said, was so great as to have caused his illness by reason of his displeasure at Madame de Chevreuse's conduct towards him. He expatiated in a long and querulous harangue upon the actions of Madame de Chevreuse, particularly respecting M. de Châteauneuf, and concluded by saying that he could no longer entertain his present sentiments for Madame de Chevreuse if she did not express her friendship for him differently from her past manner; to which Madame de Chevreuse replied that she had always endeavored to give the cardinal reason to be satisfied with her, and that she was now more anxious to please him than ever. The cardinal pressed Madame de Chevreuse in the strongest manner to discover how M. de Châteauneuf stood with her, saying that every one believed them to be extremely intimate, which I positively denied. I will say no more to you now, but believe that I esteem you as much as I despise him, and that I shall never have any secrets from M. de Châteauneuf, nor any confidence for the cardinal.

"I sacredly confirm the promise that I made you. If I have seemed to hesitate, it was not because I had since changed my mind, but merely to see if you were firm in yours. It is true that on this occasion you ask of me that which I desire to grant in order to make you more culpable if you fail in it, and me more excusable in what I shall have done.

"Should your affection be as perfect as is the ring you have sent me, you will never have cause to blush for having made an unworthy gift to your master, nor he for having received one from you.

"I share in the regret of departing without seeing you. My hatred of the cardinal's tyranny exceeds your own, but I wish to surmount rather than complain of it, since that would be the result of courage, and this of weakness. Never have I wished to converse with you so much as at this moment. The cardinal declares that Madame de Chevreuse will soon be on ill terms with you, and that M. de Châteauneuf does not love Madame de Chevreuse, and ridicules her with 47, (some unknown lady, perhaps Madame de Puisieux, whom Châteauneuf had long loved.) About her, I am in no concern; I believe M. de Châteauneuf faithful and affectionate to me, and shall be so to him through my whole life, provided that, as he has merited the good opinion which I have formed of him, he does not hereafter give me cause to lose it. I am in despair at not being able to send you to-day the picture of Madame de Chevreuse which I promised you.

"You have pledged yourself to many things, but it is necessary that you should know that the slightest failure will displease me exceedingly. Beware, therefore, of what you promise. It would be dishonorable to you if your actions did not conform to your words, and shameful to me if I suffered it. I say to you once more that you should not pledge yourself to so much if you are not well assured that you will never fail in it. I require but little where I do not expect all; but when you have promised this to me, and I have accepted the promise, I shall not be satisfied if there is the least reserve.

"I counsel you, being as yet unable to command and wishing no longer to advise you, to wear the diamond which I send you, so that on seeing the stone which has two peculiarities, one, of being firm, the other, so brilliant that it shows the slightest defects from afar, you may remember that you must be unshaken in your promises in order to please me, and must be guilty of no faults that I may not remark any.

"The cardinal is in a better humor towards Madame de Chevreuse than he has been since his return. He wrote to me this evening that he was extremely troubled about my illness, that all the favors of the king failed to give him pleasure while I remained in my present condition, and that the gayety of M. de Châteauneuf had convinced him that he bore no love to Madame de Chevreuse; that he had heard of her illness without concern; and that if Madame de Chevreuse had seen his air, she would have thought him the most dissembling, or the most unfeeling man in the world, and could never have loved him, or believed in him again. As to this, Madame de Chevreuse promises M. de Châteauneuf that, instead of being governed by the cardinal's advice, she will both love him and believe in him forever.

"I believe that M. de Châteauneuf fully belongs to Madame de Chevreuse, and I promise you that Madame de Chevreuse will ever regard M. de Châteauneuf as her own. Though all the world should neglect M. de Châteauneuf, Madame de Chevreuse will continue to esteem him so highly through her whole life that, if he loves her as truly as he has said, he will have reason to be content with his fortune, for all the powers of earth could not make me change my resolution. I swear this to you, and command you to believe it, and to love me faithfully.

"Last evening the cardinal sent to inquire after the health of Madame de Chevreuse, and wrote to her that he was dying to see her, and that he had many things to say to her, being more than ever devoted to Madame de Chevreuse, who sets little value on this protestation, but much on that which M. de Châteauneuf has made of being wholly hers. To-morrow I will tell you more. Love your master always; he is ill, and has only gone out when obliged for the last two days, but in whatever state he may be, and whatever may happen to him, he will die rather than fail in any thing he has promised you.

"At six o'clock last evening, the Cardinal de La Valette came to see Madame de Chevreuse on the part of the Cardinal de Richelieu. He addressed her sadly and submissively in behalf of his master. After this, he paid a forced admiration to Madame de Chevreuse, and offered a thousand gallantries which seemed insults to me. I answered him civilly and coldly. 37 is in despair; he says that he will destroy himself since Madame de Chevreuse will not see him; that the life which he has only cherished in the belief that it would one day be acceptable and useful to Madame de Chevreuse will henceforth be a burden to him; that having lost all hope he has lost the wish to live, and that this will be the last importunity that I shall receive from him. I hope that your affection is proof against every thing. I ask this favor of you, that it may be so, and promise you that as long as Madame de Chevreuse shall live, you shall receive the same love from her. This letter was commenced yesterday. The Cardinal de La Valette has since sent me a thousand compliments in behalf of the Cardinal de Richelieu.

"There is no means of saying any thing more about the diamond; but though the cardinal suspects Madame de Chevreuse, she will either remove his suspicions, or replace them by the conviction that all his prosperity cannot influence Madame de Chevreuse so far as to make her submit to the caprices of his whimsical humor. Do not disquiet yourself about this affair, but rather think of the health of your master who is ill and confined to his bed, for if you lose him, you will never find his like in fidelity and affection.

"I wish to see you as much as you do to converse with me, but I am troubled to find the means of doing so, because the cardinal must not know that we have met if we would not completely unhinge him. Send me word then how I must manage to see you without the knowledge of the cardinal.

"I shall always command you except this once, when I ask a favor of you, which is the greatest that you can grant me; it is that M. de Châteauneuf shall never suspect Madame de Chevreuse, but shall rest assured that he will never lose the good graces of his master until Madame de Chevreuse shall lose her life, which she hopes will not happen until she has first proved to M. de Châteauneuf how much he is esteemed by Madame de Chevreuse, though this may be more than she has promised him. But a good master never fears to err in obliging his servant, when he has proved himself full of fidelity and affection. The cardinal wishes to persuade Madame de Chevreuse that his heart is filled with both for her who will not believe his words. I would give my life to talk with you, but I know not how to manage this, for the cardinal must not know it. Consult with the bearer respecting the means for it, and believe that nothing but death can take away the sentiments that I feel for you.

"Never has there been any thing like the extravagance of the cardinal. He has written and sent the strangest complaints to Madame de Chevreuse. He says that she has constantly ridiculed him to Germain, (Lord Jermyn, the agent and particular friend of the Queen of England,) that he might tell in his own country of the contempt in which she holds him; that he knows for a certainty that Madame de Chevreuse and M. de Châteauneuf are in correspondence, and that your servants are constantly in my house; that I receive Brion because he is his enemy, in order to displease him; that everybody says that he is in love with me, and that he will no longer endure such conduct. Such is the state of the cardinal's mind. Send me word what you think of all this, but feign to know nothing of it. I shall see the cardinal here, and will inform you of all that passes. Believe that whatever may happen to your master, he will do nothing that is unworthy of himself, or which shall cause you to blush for belonging to him. I am a little better in health, and more than ever resolved to esteem M. de Châteauneuf till death, as I have promised you."

What was not the rage of the proud and imperious cardinal when he acquired certain proof that he had thus been deceived by a woman and betrayed by a friend! His vengeance fell heavily upon the two guilty ones. The only one of their accomplices whom he could reach, the Chevalier de Jars, was thrown into the Bastille and condemned to lose his head; he ascended the scaffold and there received his pardon.[1] The Marquis de Hauterive, brother of the keeper of the seals, es-

[1] Madame de Motteville, vol. i., pp. 62–69.

caped with difficulty under cover of the night and took refuge in Holland. His nephew, the Marquis de Leuville, was arrested and confined for a long time in prison, and he himself was conducted to the citadel of Angoulême, where he remained ten years, while Madame de Chevreuse, treated more gently by the cardinal, who had still a remnant of hope, received for her sole punishment an order to retire to Dampierre. But the queen could not dispense with her society, and the two friends often wished to meet to console each other by talking about their troubles, and probably, also, to devise the means of ending them. Often, under cover of the evening twilight, Madame de Chevreuse came in disguise to Paris, was secretly introduced into the Louvre or the Val-de-Grâce, saw the queen, and returned at midnight to Dampierre. But these clandestine visits were soon discovered, or at least suspected, and the faithful and daring confidant of Anne of Austria was banished to Touraine to an estate of her first husband.

One can easily imagine the mortal ennui which overwhelmed the beautiful duchess, thus buried at thirty-three in the heart of a province, far from the noise and the splendor of Paris, far from all the emotions which were so dear to her, far from all intrigues both of politics and of love. It was but a dull amusement to her to turn the head of the old Archbishop of Tours,[1] and to sustain herself she had great need of the visits of the young and amiable La Rochefoucauld,[2] who lived

---

[1] La Rochefoucauld, *Memoires*, p. 355. He was called Bertrand de Chaux, or D'Eschaux. He must have been then more than eighty years old, for we read in the Gazette of the year 1641, No. 619, p. 315, "Sieur D'Eschaux, Archbishop of Tours, Commander of the Order of Saint Esprit, and first Almoner to the King, died on the 1st of May at his Archiepiscopal palace of Tours, aged eighty-six."

[2] La Rochefoucauld, ibid., p. 355: "Madame de Chevreuse was at that time an exile in Tours. The queen had spoken well of me to her; she wished to see me, and we soon formed a strong league of friendship. I was often charged by both with dangerous commissions when going or returning."

in her neighborhood, and of the letters of Queen Anne. She remained at Tours four long years, from 1633 to the middle of 1637, employing her leisure and activity in concocting a mysterious correspondence between the queen, Charles IV., the Queen of England, and the King of Spain.

What was the real nature of this correspondence? Hitherto, all that we have known with certainty has been that it furnished food for the gravest accusations against the queen and Madame de Chevreuse. In this correspondence, the queen availed herself of the services of one of her valets de chambre, named La Porte. Sometimes, too, she retired to the Val-de-Grâce under the pretence of offering prayers, and there wrote letters which the superior, Louise de Milley, Mother de Saint Etienne, doubly devoted to Anne of Austria both as a Catholic and a Spaniard,[1] undertook to forward to their address. The queen and her friends believed themselves acting under an impenetrable disguise; but the police of the suspicious cardinal were on the alert. A note of Anne to Madame de Chevreuse, which had been confided by La Porte to a man of whom he believed himself sure, but who betrayed him, was intercepted; and La Porte was arrested, thrown into a dungeon of the Bastille, and examined in turn by the most skilful agents of the cardinal, Laffemas and La Poterie, by the chancellor, Pierre Séguier, and by Richelieu himself. At the same time, the chancellor, accompanied by the Archbishop of Paris, ordered the gates of the Val-de-Grâce to be opened, searched the cell of the queen, seized all her papers, and examined the superior, the Mother de Saint Etienne, after

---

[1] *Gallia Christiana*, vol. viii., p. 584. The Mother de Saint Etienne was abbess from 1626 until the 13th of August, 1637, when she was forced to resign, and was succeeded by Marie de Burges, Mother de Saint Benoit. She was born in Franche-Compté, and her whole family were in the service of Spain; her brother was even governor of Besançon.

having commanded her through the archbishop to speak the truth in the name of the obedience which she owed to him, and under penalty of excommunication. The queen also had much to endure, and was in great danger. Let us hear La Rochefoucauld, who ought to be correctly informed, since he was at that time, with Madame de Hautefort and Madame de Chevreuse, the most intimate confidant of Anne of Austria: "The queen was accused of having had a correspondence with the Marquis de Mirabel, Minister of Spain. This was construed into an offence against the state. Several of her domestics were arrested, and her caskets were seized. The chancellor examined her as a criminal; it was proposed to imprison her at Havre, to dissolve her marriage, and to repudiate her. In this extremity, abandoned by every one, destitute of all aid, and daring to confide in no one but Madame de Hautefort and me, she proposed to me to fly with them to Brussels. Whatever were the difficulties and dangers involved in such a project, I can truly say that it gave me the greatest joy of my life. I was then at the age in which one has a passion for brilliant and adventurous deeds, and I could conceive of none more daring than to carry away the queen from her husband and from the Cardinal de Richelieu, who was jealous of her, and at the same time to take away Madame de Hautefort from the king, who was enamored with her. Happily, affairs changed, the queen was found not guilty, the examination of the chancellor justified her, and Madame D'Aiguillon pacified the Cardinal de Richelieu."

All this story seems to us very suspicious. We do not for a moment believe that the queen ever entertained the insane idea which La Rochefoucauld attributes to her; he mistook a pleasantry of Madame de Hautefort for a serious proposition, and relates it here according to his custom to give himself an air of importance. Besides, whatever he may say, he was not daring enough to undertake so rash an enterprise; and we shall see that he was exceedingly circumspect on much less perilous occasions. The chancellor never required the queen to submit to an examination; the royal dignity positively forbade this; besides, the queen was not then in Paris, neither was she at the Val de Grâce when the chancellor visited it; she was with the king at Chantilly, and every thing was arranged by confidential explanations between the king, the queen, and Richelieu, without the intervention of the chief justice. The examination of the chancellor did not, therefore, justify the queen, nor was she acquitted; far from that, she was proved, and even acknowledged herself to be guilty, and it was to this confession that she owed the pardon which was granted her. Madame de Motteville explicitly declares this, when vindicating the innocence of her mistress, according to her usual custom. "The queen,"[1] says she, "could only obtain her pardon by signing with her own hand an acknowledgment that she had been guilty of all the things of which she had been accused, and she asked it of the king in the most humble and submissive terms. . . Every one believed her to be innocent. She was so, in truth, as far as the king was concerned; but she was guilty if it were a crime to have written to her brother and to Madame de Chevreuse. La Porte, the servant of the queen, has himself related to me the particulars of this story. He recounted it to me at a time when he was in disgrace, and therefore dissatisfied with this princess, and what he told me is worthy of credence. He was arrested on the charge of being the bearer of letters of the queen, both to Spain and to Madame de Chevreuse. He was examined three times in the Bastille by La Poterie. The Cardinal de Richelieu wished to question him himself in the presence of the chancellor. He ordered him to be brought to his house into his own chamber, where he was questioned and cross-questioned upon all the points upon which they desired to confound the queen. He remained firm and avowed nothing . . refusing the gifts and rewards

---

[1] *Memoires*, vol. i., p. 80.

which they proffered him, and choosing rather to die than to accuse the queen of crimes of which he said she was innocent. The Cardinal de Richelieu admiring his fidelity, yet persuaded that he did not speak truly, wished that he might be happy enough to have as faithful a servant as this man. A letter of the queen, written in cypher, was also discovered, and was shown her. She could not but acknowledge it; and, in order to prevent any discrepancy, it was necessary to report to La Porte this avowal of the queen that he might confirm it. It was on this occasion that Madame de Hautefort, who was still in the court, generously resolving to sacrifice herself to save the queen, disguised herself as a waiting maid, and went to the Bastille to convey a letter to La Porte, which she succeeded in doing at much risk and danger to herself, through the adroitness of the Commander de Jars, then a prisoner there. He was an adherent of the queen, and had gained over many of the people of the place, who conveyed the letter to the hands of La Porte. It apprised him of what the queen had confessed, so that being again examined by Laffemas and menaced with the question ordinary and extraordinary, he feigned to be terrified, and said that if they would send him some officer of the queen, who was a trustworthy man, he would confess all that he knew. Laffemas, believing that he had gained him, told him that he might name any one whom he chose, who would, doubtless, be sent to him. La Porte asked for one named Larivière, an officer of the queen, whom he knew to be a friend of Laffemas, and whom he really distrusted; this offer Laffemas accepted with joy. The king and the cardinal immediately sent for Larivière, and commanded him to go to La Porte without seeing the queen, and persuaded by their promises, he agreed to do all that they wished. He was taken to the Bastille, where he commanded La Porte, in the name of the queen, to reveal all that he knew concerning her affairs. La Porte feigned to believe that the queen had sent him, and told him with much hesitation all that the queen had before confessed, protesting that this was all he knew. The Cardinal de Richelieu was confounded and the king satisfied. La Porte, who is a worthy and honest man, has assured me that, having seen the letters in question, and knowing their contents, he was astonished that accusations could be formed from them against the queen, as they simply consisted of sarcasms against the Cardinal de Richelieu, and certainly said nothing against the king or the state." La Porte, in his *Memoires*,[1] confirms this recital of Madame de Motteville; he declares that there was no "finesse" in the correspondence of the queen and Madame de Chevreuse, and that the whole affair was concerted, in order "to entangle Madame de Chevreuse in it, and to make the public believe it was a dangerous cabal against the state; for it was the custom of his eminence to make trifling matters pass for great conspiracies."

It remains to be discovered whether these were, in truth, but "trifling matters," as La Porte asserts. We have listened to the testimony of friends of the queen and of Madame de Chevreuse, but we must also hear Richelieu;[2] above all, we must hear those witnesses which are more reliable than all the "Memoirs;" namely, the original and authentic documents of which Richelieu has written, and which have escaped all the historians except Père Griffet, who, in this affair as in that of Châteauneuf, gathered every thing, sifted every thing, and then, with the documents in his hand, justified the cardinal. Thanks to these documents, which we too have studied,[3]

---

[1] *Memoires*, p. 358, etc.

[2] *Memoires*, vol. x., p. 195, etc.

[3] These precious documents passed from the casket of the Cardinal de Richelieu into the library of the marshal of the same name, who transmitted them to Père Griffet, as he had formerly done the papers of Châteauneuf. The National Library has recently acquired them, *Supplement Français*, No. 4068, with the following title: *Pièces relatives à l'affaire du Val de Grâce*, 1637.

every disguise is removed; we read clearly the conduct of Anne of Austria; we see, with all deference to La Rochefoucauld, Madame de Motteville, and La Porte, that she was certainly guilty, and that Madame de Chevreuse was probably her principal accomplice, since she had continued to be as firmly leagued with her during her exile in Touraine as at the time that she was superintendent of her household.

Against Madame de Chevreuse, neither whose person nor papers were seized, there were merely presumptions—but these were very strong presumptions. La Porte, the valet de chambre of the queen, and the avowed bearer of the most of her letters, belonged to Madame de Chevreuse as much as to the queen herself, and even had a room at the Hotel de Chevreuse, which served him as a retreat. The duchess, before her departure to Tours in 1633, went twice, privately, from Dampierre to the Val de Grâce, where she had an interview with Anne of Austria. Lord Montagu, the well-known agent of the Queen of England and the intimate friend of Madame de Chevreuse, had also seen the queen once at the Val de Grâce. The courageous exile had proposed to her royal friend to break her ban and to come in disguise to meet her in Paris. She constantly corresponded with the Duke of Lorraine, and had but lately received an envoy from him. It is difficult to believe that so many intrigues had no other end in view than to learn news of the health of the queen. Upon this point the proofs are direct; we have her own avowals, signed by her own hand. It is very probable that she has not told all, but what she has told proves that she had written several times to Spain and to Flanders, that is to say, to hostile countries, not only to complain of her situation, but also to impart and reveal the most important secrets of the French government. 1st. She had informed the court at Madrid of the journey of a monk who had been sent to Spain on a secret mission. 2d. She had given notice that France was endeavoring to make terms with the Duke of Lorraine, in order that the cabinet at

Madrid might take measures to hinder this adjustment. 3d. She had also informed them that there was reason to fear that England, instead of remaining allied to Spain, would break the league and enter into a treaty with France.

It seems to us either that crimes of state have ceased to exist in the world, or else that they are manifest in this affair. We see that it was with infinite pains that Anne of Austria had been brought to make these avowals. At first she denied every thing, and said that if she had written several times to Madame de Chevreuse, it had always been on indifferent matters. On Assumption day, after receiving the sacrament, she sent for her secretary, Le Gras, and swore to him by the Holy Communion, which she had just received, that it was false that she had had a correspondence with a foreign country, and commanded him to go tell the cardinal the oath she had just made. She also sent for Father Caussin, a Jesuit and confessor to the king, and renewed the same oath to him. Two days afterwards, finding that it was impossible to maintain so absolute a denial, she commenced by confessing to Richelieu that she had really written to Flanders to her brother, the Infant Cardinal, but merely to inquire after his health, and to ask about other matters of little importance. Richelieu having convinced her that he knew more than this, she ordered her maid of honor, Madame de Sénecé, Chavigny, and de Noyers, who were present, to withdraw, and, being left alone with the cardinal, upon the assurance that he would obtain a full and unconditional pardon from the king if she confessed the truth, she acknowledged all, exhibiting extreme confusion in respect to her false oaths. During this humiliating confession, calling to her aid the graces and arts of her sex, and concealing her real feelings beneath feigned demonstrations, she repeatedly exclaimed, "What goodness you must possess, M. le Cardinal!" Then, protesting an eternal gratitude, she said to him, "Give me your hand," at the same time presenting her own as a pledge of her sincerity; but the cardinal respectfully refused it, drawing back instead of approaching her.[1] The Abbess of Val de Grâce followed the example of the queen; after having denied all, she confessed every thing. The king and Richelieu pardoned them, but forced the queen to sign a sort of schedule of conduct to which she should scrupulously conform. They provisionally interdicted her entrance to the Val de Grâce, as well as to every other convent, until the king should again give her permission to visit them; they forbade her to write except in the presence of her first maid of honor and first waiting maid, who should render an account of it to the king; or to address a single letter to a foreign country, by any direct or indirect means, under penalty of the forfeiture of the pardon which they had accorded her. Both the first and the last of these prohibitions related to the duchess. The king ordered his wife never to write to Madame de Chevreuse, "because this pretext," said he, "has been the cover of all the letters which the queen has written beside." He also commanded her neither to see Craft, an English gentleman and a friend of Montagu and the duchess, who was strongly suspected of being mixed up in all their intrigues, nor "any of the other agents of Madame de Chevreuse." We see, then, that it is always Madame de Chevreuse whom Louis XIII. and Richelieu regard as the root of all evil, and that they do not believe themselves sure of the queen until after having first separated her from her dangerous friend.

But how must this be done? Should they leave her at Tours? or arrest her? or banish her from France? It is curious to see what were the deliberations of the cardinal on this question, both with himself and with the king. He involuntarily renders striking homage to the power of Madame de Chevreuse by proving by a series of reasons, somewhat scholastically deducted after his usual manner, that the worst

[1] *Memoires* of Richelieu, vol. x., p. 201.

course of all would be to suffer her to quit France. "This spirit is so dangerous, that, being abroad, she may bring affairs into new disorder which it is impossible to foresee. It is she, who, having absolute disposal of the Duke of Lorraine, has persuaded him to give an asylum in his territory to Monsieur, the Duke of Orleans; and it is also she who has urged on England to war; if she is thrust from the kingdom, she will hinder the Duke of Lorraine from coming to terms; she will incite the English towards the point to which she wishes to carry them; she will agitate new schemes in favor of the Chevalier de Jars and Châteauneuf; she will stir up a thousand troubles within and without;"[1] and the cardinal concluded to retain her in France.

For this there were two courses open, violence and gentleness. The cardinal showed many objections to violence, which would certainly be followed by importunate solicitations on the part of all the family of Madame de Chevreuse, together with all the powers of Europe, which it would be difficult long to resist. He proposed, therefore, to win her over by kindness, and to treat her as they had treated the queen, but on condition that she should be as frank as Anne had been, and should answer all the questions that might be addressed to her; but, knowing Madame de Chevreuse, he must have foreseen that she would make no confession, and he forgets to tell us what he should then have done. They had pardoned the humbled and repentant queen, but what course would they have pursued with the proud and artful duchess, persisting in an absolute denial? Satisfied with having separated her from Anne of Austria, would Richelieu have left her free and tranquil in Touraine? Is he really sincere when he affirms it, or is the old charm still acting, and is this iron heart, this inexorable soul, which beauty, however, more than once found impressible, unable to shield itself from a re-

[1] *Memoires*, p. 224, etc.

luctant tenderness for a woman who joined in her person in the highest degree, those two gifts so rarely found united—beauty and courage?

He spoke to her as if he were still her friend; he reminded her of the leniency which he had shown her in the affair of Châteauneuf; and, knowing her to be at that time almost destitute, he sent her money. The duchess made much ceremony about receiving it; she would not take it as a gift, but as a loan; and the only favor which she asked of the cardinal was that of assistance in the just suit which she was prosecuting in order to separate her property from that of her husband—a suit which she gained some time afterward. The questions which were addressed to her, she answered without embarrassment and with her usual firmness. Unable to deny that she had proposed to the queen to return in disguise to Paris, since they had seized the letter in which the queen had declined the proposition, she declared that she had had no other desire in this than to have the honor of saluting her sovereign; that the urgency of her affairs had also called her to Paris; and that, far from thinking to animate the queen against the cardinal, her intention had been to employ all the influence which she might have possessed over her in disposing her favorably towards the prime minister; and, paying Richelieu in his own coin, she gave him back his professions of friendship with interest; but, in her heart, she distrusted him. It was in vain that the envoys of Richelieu, the Marshal La Meilleraie, the Bishop of Auxerre, and above all the Abbé du Dorat, treasurer of Sainte-Chapelle, with whom she was on friendly terms, said every thing that they could imagine to persuade her of the sincerity of the cardinal; she only saw in this assiduous friendliness a skilful plan designed to lull her vigilance, and to inspire her with a false security. She thought of her friends, the Chevalier de Jars and Châteauneuf, both languishing in the dungeons of Richelieu, and resolved to brave all dangers rather than share their fate.

In the mean time, Anne of Austria had early felt the need, for her own safety, of acquainting Madame de Chevreuse with all that had passed; and, having promised to hold no intercourse with her, she charged La Rochefoucauld, who was going to Poitou, to tell her what she dared not write to her herself. La Rochefoucauld had just made the same promise to his father and Chavigny, a confidant of the cardinal, and he who pretends that he would gladly have carried off the queen and Madame de Hautefort, paused with admirable scrupulousness before the pledge he had just given, and begged Craft, the English gentleman who was so much suspected by the king and by Richelieu, to execute the queen's commission. On her part, Madame de Hautefort had despatched one of her relatives, M. de Montalais, to Tours, when affairs were at their crisis, to inform Madame de Chevreuse of the real state of things, and to tell her that she would send her a prayer-book bound in green if affairs took a favorable turn, while a prayer-book bound in red should be a token that she must hasten to provide for her safety. A fatal contempt of the sign agreed on, together with a profound distrust of the designs of Richelieu and the king, hurried Madame de Chevreuse into a desperate resolve. She chose rather to condemn herself to a new exile than to run the risk of falling into the hands of her enemies, and fled from Touraine, determining to reach Spain by journeying through the whole of the South of France.

Her sole confidant was her old admirer, the Archbishop of Tours. As he was from Bearn and had relatives on the frontier, he gave her letters of introduction with all necessary information respecting the different roads which she should take. But in her haste to fly, she forgot them all, and set out on the 6th of September, 1637,[1] in a carriage, as if to take an

---

[1] Extract from the *Information faite par le président Vignier de la sortie faite par Madame de Chevreuse hors de France*, with various corroborative papers. BIBLIOTHÈQUE NATIONALE, *Coll. Du Puy*, Nos. 499 500, and 501, collected in a single volume.

airing; then, at nine in the evening, she mounted on horseback disguised as a man, and, when five or six leagues from home, found herself without letters, without itinerary, without waiting-maid, and followed only by two servants. She was unable to change her horse during the night, and she arrived the next morning at Ruffec, one league from Verteuil, where La Rochefoucauld resided, without having taken a single hour of repose. Instead of claiming his hospitality, she wrote him the following note: "Sir, I am a French gentleman who asks your aid to preserve his liberty, and perhaps his life. I have fought an unhappy duel, and have killed a nobleman of distinction. This forces me to leave France in haste, as I am pursued. I believe you to be generous enough to serve me without knowing me. I need a carriage and a valet to attend me." La Rochefoucauld sent her what she wished. The carriage was a great relief to her, for she was worn out with fatigue. Her new guide conducted her to another house of Rochefoucauld, where she arrived at midnight; there she left the carriage and the two domestics who had hitherto accompanied her, and again set out on horseback towards the frontier of Spain. The saddle of her horse was covered with blood; this she said was from a sword thrust she had received in the thigh. She slept in a barn on the hay, and scarcely tasted food. But as beautiful and as fascinating in the black costume of a cavalier as in the brilliant attire of a court lady, her gallant mien won the admiration of all the women, and during this adventurous journey, she made, despite herself, as many conquests as when in the halls of the Louvre, and, according to La Rochefoucauld, "she showed more modesty and more cruelty than men like her usually possess."[1] At one time she met ten or twelve cava-

[1] La Rochefoucauld, p. 356. Tallemant, Vol. i., p. 250, relates the strangest imaginable anecdotes, but we shall only cite certain and authentic facts. *Extrait de l'information*, etc.: A citizen's wife passed by chance, and seeing her lying on the hay, exclaimed: "This is the hand-

liers commanded by the Marquis D'Antin, and was obliged to turn aside from her route to avoid being recognized by them. Another time, in a valley of the Pyrenees, a gentleman who had seen her in Paris, told her that he should take her for Madame de Chevreuse if she were dressed in a different manner, but the fair unknown extricated herself from this difficulty by replying that, being a relative of that lady, she might well resemble her. Her courage and gayety did not abandon her for a moment, and, to portray the valiant Amazon, a song was made in which she says to her squire:

> La Boissière, dis-moi
> Vais-je pas bien en homme?
> Vous chevauchez, ma foi,
> Mieux que tant que nous sommes, etc.[1]

Her attendant urging her to acquaint him with her name, she told him in a mysterious manner that she was the Duke D'Enghien, who was forced by especial business in the service of the king to quit France in this manner; which may give us an idea of her appearance on horseback, as well as of her resolute and decided air. Afterwards, gaining confidence in her guide, and disliking long to wear a mask, she confessed to him that she was the Duchess de Chevreuse. She only reached Spain after enduring unheard-of fatigue, and passing through a thousand perils.[2] Just before crossing the frontier, she wrote to the gentleman who had fancied that he recognized her in the Pyrenees, and who had shown her every attention and civility, that he had not been mistaken, but that she was really the lady whom he had believed her to be, and that, "having found

somest youth I ever saw! Sir, come rest in my house, you excite my pity," etc.

[1] Tallemant, ibid.

[2] *Extrait de l'information:* Malbasty told her that she would lose her way, that she would meet a host of robbers, that she had but a single man with her, and that he feared some one would harm her. She offered a large rouleau of pistoles to the said Malbasty.

him unusually courteous, she took the liberty of entreating him to procure her stuffs to clothe herself conformably to her sex and condition.[1] Having at last reached Spain, with her accustomed resolution she threw herself for a second time into the hardships of exile, taking nothing with her but her beauty, her talent, and her courage. She had sent one of her servants to La Rochefoucauld with all her jewels—valued at 200,000 crowns—entreating him to accept them as a legacy if she should die, or else to restore them to her at some future day.

At the news of the flight of Madame de Chevreuse, Richelieu was greatly disturbed, and he used every effort to hinder her departure from France. The strictest orders were instantly issued, not to arrest, but to detain her. M. de Chevreuse sent his steward, M. de Boispille in search of his wife with the assurance that she had nothing to fear. The cardinal also despatched President Vignier, one of his trusty friends, with a full permission to reside in perfect liberty at Tours, together with the hope of a speedy return to Dampièrre. At the same time, Vignier was ordered to question the old archbishop as well as La Rochefoucauld and his people, and to extract from them all the information that could be of use to the minister.[2] But neither Boispille nor Vignier could overtake the beautiful fugitive, and she had just touched the soil of Spain when the president reached the frontier. He wished, however, to execute his commission as fully as he could, and sent a herald on the Spanish territory to convey to Madame de Chevreuse a pardon for the past and an invitation to return to France. She did not learn of all these proceedings until she was already in Madrid.

---

[1] La Rochefoucauld, *Memoirès*, ibid.

[2] These are the documents which Du Puy has collected or rather abridged, and of which we have availed ourselves to verify our narrative, using also the account of Richelieu and that of La Rochefoucauld. It was on this occasion that La Rochefoucauld was thrown for eight days into the Bastille. See his *Memoires*, together with *La Jeunesse de Mme. de Longueville*, third edition, chap. iv., p. 279, etc.

CHAPTER II

1637–1643.

Madame de Chevreuse in Spain, and in England.—Long negotiation with Richelieu to return to France.—Failure of the negotiation.—Marie de Medicis and the Duke d'Épernon.—Madame de Chevreuse in Flanders.—Conspiracy and rebellion of Count de Soissons.—Affair of Cinq-Mars.—Death of Richelieu and of Louis XIII.—Royal declaration of the 20th of April, 1643, condemning Madame de Chevreuse to a perpetual exile.—Her recall by the new regent.

We can easily imagine the reception which the King of Spain gave the intrepid friend of his royal sister. He sent several carriages-and-six to meet her, and at Madrid he overwhelmed her with every mark of honor. Madame de Chevreuse was then thirty-seven years of age. To her many attractions she added the prestige of the romantic adventures which she had just passed through, and it is said that Philip IV. swelled the list of her conquests.[1] She was already thoroughly English, and thoroughly Lorraine; she soon became Spanish also. She leagued herself with the Count-Duke Olivares, and gained a powerful ascendency over the councils of the cabinet at Madrid. This she doubtless owed to her talent and brilliancy, and still more to the noble pride which she displayed in refusing the pensions and money that were offered her, and in always speaking of France in a manner befitting the former Constabless de Luynes.[2]

---

[1] Madame de Motteville, vol. i., p. 93.

[2] Bibliothèque Nationale, *Manuscrits de Colbert, affaires de France*, in folio. Vol. ii., fol. 9. *Mémoire de ce que Madame de Chevreuse a donné charge au sieur de Boispille de dire a monseigneur le cardinal.* "She incurred no obligations in Spain, and would not accept a tester

Notwithstanding, whatever pleasure the declared favor of the king, the queen, and the prime minister may have given her in Spain, she did not remain long there. The war between the two countries rendered her position very delicate, her letters penetrated with difficulty into France, and her friends dared not write to her, so much did they dread the police of Richelieu, and so much did they fear being accused of corresponding with the enemy, and with Madame de Chevreuse. Even Boispille, her steward, on receiving a letter from her, said to the messenger, who asked for an answer: "We make no answers to Spain." To have more liberty, and to be nearer France, she resolved to go to a neutral and even friendly country, and in the commencement of the year 1638, she arrived in England.

Madame de Chevreuse was received and treated in London as she had been before in Madrid. She found there her earliest admirer, Count Holland, Lord Montagu, who was still enamoured with her, Craft,[1] and many other noblemen, both English and French, who hastened to swell her train. She especially charmed the king and queen. She had always been a favorite with Charles I., and Henriette, on again beholding the chaperon who had escorted her to her royal husband, embraced her, and invited her to be seated in her presence, an unusual mark of distinction in the court of England.

The king and queen wrote in her behalf to Louis XIII., to Queen Anne, and to Cardinal de Richelieu. Madame de Chevreuse demanded the full and entire enjoyment of her property, which had once been granted her, and then withdrawn after her flight to Spain. In the spring of 1638, the

---

with the exception of good cheer and treatment. . . . . She spoke as befitted her in Spain, and believed that this was one thing that made the count-duke esteem her."

[1] *Memoirs* of Richelieu, vol. x., p. 488.

pregnancy of Queen Anne becoming public, filled the French court with joy, and inspired every heart with hope. Madame de Chevreuse profited by this event to address the following letter to the queen, which she could show without hesitation to Louis XIII., but which, notwithstanding its reserve and diplomatic circumspection, discloses the warm and reciprocal affection of the queen and the exile:[1]

"*To the queen, my sovereign lady:*

"Madame, I should be unworthy of pardon if I had been able to render an account to your Majesty of the journey which my misfortunes obliged me to undertake, and had failed to do so. But necessity having constrained me to enter Spain, where respect for your Majesty caused me to be received and treated better than I merited, the duty which I owed you compelled me to keep silent until I should be in a kingdom whose alliance with France would not give me cause to apprehend that you would be displeased at receiving letters from it. This one will speak first of all of the great joy which I feel at the pregnancy of your Majesty. May God console and reward all who belong to her[2] by this happiness, which I entreat him with all my heart to complete by the happy accouchement of a dauphin. Although my unhappy fortune hinders me from being among the first to witness it, believe that my devotion to the service of your Majesty will not let me be among the last to rejoice at it. The memory which your Majesty doubtless retains of what I owe to her, and my own remembrance of what I wish to render to her, is sufficient to convince her of the grief it has been to me to see myself obliged to quit her, in order to escape the troubles into which I feared that unjust suspicions

---

[1] *Manuscrits de Colbert*, ibid.

[2] It is hardly necessary to remind the reader that, in all French letters addressed to sovereigns, the feminine pronoun *her* is used instead of the pronoun you, of course referring to your *Majesty*."—Tr.

might plunge me. It has been necessary for me to deprive myself of the consolation of assuaging my sorrows by telling them to your Majesty, until the present hour, when I can complain to her of my unhappy fortune, hoping that her protection will shelter me from the anger of the king and the dislike of the cardinal. I dare not say this to his Majesty myself, and do not tell it to M. the cardinal, being assured that your generosity will do so, and thus make that agreeable which in me would be importunate. The knowledge of the kindness of your Majesty assures me that she will willingly exercise it on this occasion, and that she will employ her charity to prove to me what I already know, that she is still herself. Your Majesty will learn from the letters of the King and Queen of Great Britain the honor they do me. I do not know how better to express myself than by telling your Majesty that it merits her acknowledgment. I trust that she will approve of my residence in their court, that this will not render me deserving of any harsh treatment, and that I shall not be refused the property which the authority of your Majesty and the care of M. the cardinal had procured me before my departure, and which I demand of my husband. In which I supplicate your Majesty to protect me, so that I may soon be in possession of the just rights for which I am hoping."

At the same time that she claimed her property, Madame de Chevreuse thought of acquitting a debt which weighed heavily on her pride. At Tours she had really been forced to accept the money sent her by Richelieu, but, as we have already said,[1] she accepted it simply as a loan; and under cover of the official letter to Queen Anne, which we have just given, she enclosed a little confidential note, designed for the queen alone, from which we see that the Queen of France had herself formerly borrowed money from her ex-superintendent.

---

[1] *Manuscrits de Colbert*, ibid.

The note, in fact, besought her to pay the cardinal what was due to him, and, if she could, "to settle the balance of the debt."

These last words, with many others in subsequent letters, show us that since her departure from France, Madame de Chevreuse, being unwilling to receive any thing from a foreign power, had exhausted all her resources, and that, not having the disposal of her property, she had been compelled to contract debts in London, which were constantly increasing, and which she knew not how to satisfy. Meanwhile, M. de Chevreuse, who had reduced his affairs to the most deplorable state, and whose sole hope of retrieving them lay in his wife's good sense and influence, had been continually interceding with the king and prime minister to permit her to return to France. The cardinal renewed his offer of pardon and *abolition*, which, he said, President Vignier had already taken the trouble to carry to her to the frontiers of Spain. Besides the general reasons for wishing her return which he himself has adduced, he had a very particular one just at this moment: he was negotiating with the Duke of Lorraine, whose military talents and small but excellent army disquieted him not a little, and he was more than ever anxious to draw him into a peace which would leave him free to unite all the forces of France against Spain and Austria. He had the greatest interest, therefore, in gaining the friendship of Madame de Chevreuse, whose influence was all-powerful over the mind of the duke, and who, as he was firmly persuaded, had already foiled the desired arrangement in 1637, and had it in her power to prevent it again. On her part, Madame de Chevreuse was weary of exile; she sighed for her chateau of Dampierre,[1] and for her children,

[1] One can well imagine it, on seeing this beautiful residence, still decorated by a cultivated and refined taste. The descendant of Marie de Rohan, the Constabless de Luynes, has converted the ancient Chateau de Guise into a tasteful and splendid residence, which rivals the most celebrated palaces of the English aristocracy. Where else can we find

especially her daughter, the amiable Charlotte, who was growing up far from her mother. She shuddered at the thought of the painful alternative which each day pressed her more strongly: either of being forced to have recourse to England and Spain, or to pledge the jewels that she had reclaimed from La Rochefoucauld.[1] She clung to this rich parure, which is said to have come from Florence, from Marshal D'Ancre, as the brilliant souvenir of happier days; for Madame de Chevreuse was a woman with the weaknesses as well as the charms of her sex, and when passion and honor did not thrust her in the midst of perils, she delighted in all the elegancies of life.[2] It was this mixture of womanly gentleness with masculine energy that formed the most striking trait of her character, and that rendered her fit for every position, as well for the endearments and confidence of love as for the excitement of

---

such grandeur and simplicity, such exquisite appreciation of Nature and of Art, as is shown in these beautiful fountains, these magnificent promenades, and this vast library, these admirable family portraits, these paintings, or, rather, splendid sketches of M. Ingres, and this statue in massive silver of Louis XIII., the token of a generous gratitude? And when we reflect that he who has collected all these beautiful things, has devoted his fortune to the public good in every way, that he has given us the steel of Damascus, the ruins of Sélinonte, the history of the house of Anjou à Naples, and the Minerva of the Parthenon; that, during thirty years, he has planted asylums, schools, and hospitals everywhere about him, and encouraged and sustained scholars and artists, being himself one of the first connoisseurs and archæologists of Europe, the friend of a judicious liberty, and favorable to every good, popular cause, we may exclaim, There is one great nobleman, then, still in France!

[1] See, in respect to this, *La Jeunesse de Madame de Longueville*, third edition, chap. iv., p. 280.

[2] Madame de Chevreuse, like her grandson, loved the arts and encouraged them. She was the patroness of the excellent engraver, Pierre Daret, who dedicated to her his collection of the "*Illustres Français et estrangers de l'un et de l'autre sexe*," in quarto, 1654. This dedication acquaints us with facts that are not to be found in any of the biographies of this artist.

intrigue and adventure. It was under the influence of these varied feelings that she decided to resume a negotiation with Richelieu that had never wholly been broken off, and the successful termination of which appeared easy enough, since both parties equally wished for it.

This negotiation lasted for more than a year. The cardinal authorized Boispille, the steward of the family de Chevreuse, and Abbé du Dorat, to repair to England, the better to conduct this delicate affair. They bestowed much time and pains on it; more than once were they obliged to go from London to Paris, and from Paris to London, to smooth down the difficulties that were constantly arising. The oft-broken thread was knotted anew, but only to be again broken. The cardinal and the duchess sincerely desired to effect a reconciliation, but knowing each other well, each wished to exact from the other almost impossible pledges of fidelity. On studying the various documents to which this long negotiation gave rise,[1] we recognize therein the genius and characteristics of Richelieu and of Madame de Chevreuse; the habitual artifice of the cardinal with his ill-dissembled firmness; and the suppleness of the beautiful duchess, her apparent submission, and her inflexible precautions. Richelieu gradually relaxed his habitual rigor, but his claims—always visible through the most studied courtesy—warned Madame de Chevreuse to be on her guard, and to make no mistakes with a man who forgot nothing, and who was powerful enough for every thing. It is a curious spectacle to see them employing all the manœuvres of the most refined diplomacy, and

[1] In the *Bibliothèque Nationale* are two manuscripts which contain it entire: one, which the Père Griffet knew and profited by, is volume ii. of the *Manuscrits de Colbert*, *affaires de France;* these are but copies, and are often defective. The other, *Supplement Français*, No. 4067, contains fewer documents, but original ones, among which are several autograph letters of Richelieu and of Madame de Chevreuse.

exhausting the resources of a consummate ability for more than a year, in order to persuade and attract each other towards the common end which both desired, without succeeding in it, and without being able to cure themselves of their mutual and incurable suspicions. Let us look at the principal features—the beginning, the progress, the details, and the inevitable end of this singular correspondence.

It is opened on the 1st of June, 1638, by a letter from Madame de Chevreuse. The duchess thanks the cardinal for the friendly assurances which have been given her in his behalf; she confesses to him that, when, in the preceding year, she resolved to quit France, it was from apprehension of the suspicions which he seemed to entertain of her, and that she wished to leave to time the task of dissipating them. "I hope," she says, "that the evil fortune which constrained me to flee from France is weary of pursuing me. . . I should be very glad to be entirely cured of my fears by the discovery that my enemies are not more powerful than my innocence."[1] This letter, while feigning frankness and confidence, is exceedingly artful and reserved. Madame de Chevreuse carefully guards against engaging in any discussion upon the past, though she slightly refers to it in order to sound Richelieu, not wishing to expose herself to an investigation concerning her previous conduct on her return to France; she is therefore careful to use the word *innocence* adroitly, yet without protestation. The part Madame de Chevreuse meant to play may be understood from this first letter—it consisted in quietly procuring a pledge of her safety. To cease from declaring her innocence would have been to deliver herself into the hands of Richelieu, who, at the first feigned or real symptom of discontent, could arm himself with her confessions and crush her. The answer of the cardinal also discloses, and, as we think, a little too clearly, his secret thought; like his usual

[1] Manuscripts of Colbert, *ibid.*

policy, it is both captious and imperious. In the midst of somewhat affected demonstrations of politeness, he says to her, "That which you send me is couched in such terms that, being unable to consent to it without acting against your interests, I will make no reply to it for fear of displeasing you while wishing to serve you. In a word, madame, if you are innocent, your safety depends upon yourself, and if the frailty of human nature, to say nothing of that of your sex, has made you remiss in any thing of which his majesty may have reason to complain, you will find in his goodness all that you can expect from it." Madame de Chevreuse readily comprehended the artifice of the cardinal; but that she might leave no room for any equivocation, she addressed him a memorial in which she gave an account of all her actions, and of the reasons which had determined her to quit France. She had fled because, while lavishing fair words on her, they had endeavored to make her confess that she had written to the Duke of Lorraine in order to prevent him from breaking with Spain and entering into an arrangement with France, and being unable to confess a fault which she had never committed, and seeing that they were persuaded of it and that they even alleged intercepted letters, she had chosen to quit her country rather than remain suspected and in perpetual danger. Richelieu hastened to reassure her, but on the contrary he alarmed her, by seeming to be convinced of that which she was fully determined never to avow. Was it a judicious method of inspiring her with confidence to remind her of the affair of Châteauneuf, and plainly to intimate that he had proofs of it in his hands which would dispense with any avowal on her part? "When M. de Boispille went to seek you, I told him wherein I thought your interest and your safety lay: namely, in keeping nothing secret. I think you should the more readily assent to this, as experience has shown you by what passed in the affair of M. de Châteauneuf that, in whatever interests you, your friends are the most secret when they have the proofs in their hands. It is so difficult to induce you to confess these, where one is not sure, that when he is sure, he would almost prefer to be in ignorance, that he may not be obliged to insist upon confession."

Can we wonder after this that Madame de Chevreuse drew back, or that she was at least much embarrassed? She wrote to the cardinal on the 8th of September to express to him her gratitude for the kindness he had shown her and, at the same time, the trouble which she felt at his settled conviction that she was really guilty. Her letter admirably depicts her perplexities.

"Consider the state in which I am; well-satisfied on one hand with the assurances which you give me of the continuation of your friendship, and deeply grieved on the other by your suspicion, or rather by your alleged certainty, of a fault which I never committed, and which, I confess, would be attended with another if, having committed it, I should deny it after the pardon of the king, which you would procure me upon confession. I confess that this so embarrasses me that I see no rest for myself in this position. If you were not so certainly persuaded of knowing my fault, or if I could possibly confess it, there would be means of accommodation; but as you suffer yourself to be carried away by so strong a belief against me as to admit of no justification, and as I am unable to make myself guilty without being so, I have recourse to yourself, supplicating you in the character of friend which your generosity promises me, to propose an expedient whereby to satisfy his majesty and secure my safe return to France, being unable myself to conceive of any, and finding myself in the greatest perplexity."

Now see the expedient which Richelieu devised to free Madame de Chevreuse from the anxiety that tormented her. He sent her a royal declaration by which she was authorized

---

[1] *Manuscrits de Colbert*, letter of July 24, 1638.

to return to France with a full pardon for her past conduct, especially for her negotiations with the Duke of Lorraine against the interests of the king. On receiving this unhoped-for favor, Madame de Chevreuse protested against the pardon of a crime which she would not acknowledge at any price; only confessing herself culpable in respect to her precipitate flight from the kingdom. The means taken to dissipate her suspicions only increased them; she set about examining all the terms of this declaration with a zealous care, and she soon found ambiguity enough in that which related to her return to Dampierre. It was not said explicitly that she might remain there at full liberty. The only prohibitions to which she would consent were those of never seeing the queen, and of holding no foreign correspondence. Aside from these, she demanded a full liberty;—above all, she demanded that under a pretence of pardon she should not be charged with a fault which she pretended never to have committed.

On the 23d of February, 1639, she refused therefore the indemnity which had been sent her, and demanded an explanation of the manner in which she would be permitted to reside in France. The cardinal, irritated at seeing all his schemes discovered and eluded, flew into a passion, and disclosed the drift of his designs in a letter to the Abbé du Dorat, dated March 14th, in which he complained that Madame de Chevreuse would not acknowledge her negotiations with foreign powers, "as if," said he, "any one ever saw a sick man cured of a disease which he would not allow that he had." He did not intend to permit Madame de Chevreuse to remain longer than eight or ten days at Dampierre, after which she must retire to some one of her estates at a distance from Paris. He consented, however, to modify the royal indemnity which had so much displeased Madame de Chevreuse, and sent her another which was a little more lenient as a proof of his condescension and of the goodness of the king.

This new declaration was still very far from being what

Madame de Chevreuse desired; she was not only absolved in it from her flight from France, but "from the other faults and crimes which she might have committed against the fidelity which she owed to the king;" and Richelieu thus evasively returned to his original purpose of imposing upon the unhappy exile, indirectly at least, a confession of crimes which she maintained that she had never committed—a confession at once humiliating and dangerous, and placing her wholly at his mercy. Yet such was the desire of the poor woman to behold her country and her family that, after having a second time vainly protested against it, she resigned herself to this doubtful grace. She did more; Richelieu having hastened to remit to the Abbé du Dorat and to Boispille the money necessary to acquit the debts which she had contracted in England, and to enable her to quit that court in a style befitting her rank and dignity, she consented to permit two intermediate agents to sign in her name a writing designed to satisfy Richelieu without too deeply compromising herself, in which she humbly spoke of her past misconduct in very general terms,[1] and pledged herself never to come in secret to Paris, provided she were allowed to live in perfect freedom at Dampierre. The entreaties of the Abbé du Dorat and of Boispille, and the solemn promise which Richelieu renewed to her in a final letter of April 13th, 1639, might well have conquered her scruples, stifled her suspicions, and caused her to yield her secret instincts to the solicitations of her family.

Affairs stood in this wise; the proud duchess had bowed her head beneath the weight of exile and misfortune; she was about to depart; her adieus were already made to the Queen of England, and a vessel was ready to conduct her to Dieppe where a carriage awaited her; when suddenly, at the end of the month of April, she received the following letter, without date or signature, which we faithfully transcribe:

---

[1] Ibid.

"I should not be the friend to you that I am, if I failed to tell you that if you love Madame de Chevreuse, you will prevent her ruin, which is inevitable in France, where they only wish her for her destruction. This is not merely an opinion; there is no other remedy than that of following this advice whereby to save Madame de Chevreuse, of whose connections with Spain and M. de Lorraine, the cardinal has already spoken too ill to permit him to be silent in the future. In short, at this moment, there is nothing but patience for Madame de Chevreuse, or sure destruction to her and eternal regret to the writer."

From whatever source this note may have come, we can readily imagine that it troubled Madame de Chevreuse. It responded to all the secret instincts of her heart, and to the knowledge which she had had of old of the implacable resentment of the cardinal. She suspended or prolonged her preparations for departure; and acting as frankly as prudently, she showed the letter which she had received to Boispille, and authorized him to transmit it to the cardinal. A month had scarcely passed, ere she received another letter of the same stamp, no longer anonymous, but signed by the man of all others the most devoted to her.

"I am certain that it is the design of the cardinal to offer you every possible inducement to persuade you to return to France,—then immediately to destroy you. The Marquis de Ville, who has talked with him and with M. de Chavigny, can give you further explanations, having heard it himself. I expect him every moment, but if I thought that I had influence enough over your mind to persuade you from taking this resolution, I would hasten to throw myself at your feet to convince you of the certainty of your utter ruin, and to conjure you by all that is most dear to you to shun this calamity, too cruel to the whole world, but most of all insupportable to me; protesting that if my destruction could procure your repose, I should esteem the occasion happy which enabled me to do so; and my only motive in serving you is regard for your interest, being for ever, Madame, your most devoted servant,

"Charles de Lorraine.

"Cirk, *May* 26, 1639."

This new counsel heightened the anxiety of Madame de Chevreuse. She transmitted this second letter to Richelieu as she had done the first, to show him that she was not detained by trivial causes, and to explain to him her uncertainty. She also declared that she would not depart till she had seen and heard the Marquis de Ville whom the Duke of Lorraine had announced to her.

Henri de Livron, Marquis de Ville, was a Lorraine nobleman, full of wit and courage, and devoted to his country and his prince, who having been made prisoner, thrown into the Bastille, and afterwards released by Richelieu, had rejoined the Duke Charles in the Netherlands. He came to London in the first part of the month of August, 1639, and used every effort to persuade Madame de Chevreuse to break with the cardinal. The duchess wished that he should explain himself in the presence of Boispille, and that the latter should render an account of the interview to Richelieu. The Marquis de Ville continued inflexible in his assertions, and asked nothing better than to draw up and sign the following deposition :—"A person named Lange, having accompanied me last winter from Paris as far as Charenton, said to me that his knowledge of the interest which I had for the service of Madame de Chevreuse forced him to tell me that she was lost if she returned to France at present. Pressing him to tell me what he knew positively on the subject, after having first extracted a promise from me that I would not speak of it to any one but his Highness of Lorraine or Madame de Chevreuse, he said that it was but two days since the cardinal, in speaking of Madame de Chevreuse to M. de Chavigny, showed much dissatisfaction because she persisted in denying that she had counselled M. de Lorraine not to make terms with France. At this, M. de Chavigny also seemed very greatly surprised, and both said that the matter now was very clear, and that Madame de Chevreuse being once in France, they could make her speak plain French with the letters they possessed; that she did not believe it, but if she thought to deceive them she deceived herself. This the deponent affirms, having heard it himself. At London, this eighth day of August.

" HENRI DE LIVRON, Marquis de Ville."

This writing, as well as the preceding ones, was punctually sent to Richelieu.

We ask whether all this should not naturally have made the strongest impression on the mind of Madame de Chevreuse? Could she recall without terror the obstinate endeavors of the cardinal to draw from her by direct and indirect means a confession which could be of little importance to him, if he had no intention of using it against her? Did she not know his imperious temper, and his passion for holding the whole world at his feet, and for always having wherewith to crush his enemies? Whoever has felt the bitterness and miseries of exile will not be surprised that the unhappy duchess should have descended so far as to submit to hard and insecure conditions in her ardent desire of regaining her country and her home. But who can blame her upon such counsels as those which we have just quoted, for hesitating to take a step, which, should it prove a false one, would leave her nothing but eternal regret and useless despair.

Ere long another counsel, which was to her an order, enchained her to a foreign land. She for whom she had suffered every thing and braved every thing for the last ten years, her royal accomplice, Anne of Austria, warned her not to trust to appearances. The queen, meeting M. de Chevreuse one day at St. Germain, inquired after the duchess. He replied that he had reason to complain of her majesty, who alone hindered his wife from returning. The queen told him that he was very wrong in reproaching her;[1] that she loved Madame de Chevreuse and wished much to see her, but that she should never counsel her to return to France. It seemed to Madame de Chevreuse that Anne of Austria ought to be well informed; and she resolved to follow advice that came from so high a quarter. She would not accept the money of Richelieu, and wrote to him for the last time on the 16th of September, representing to him her uncertainty and embarrassment, and asking time to calm her fears. On the same day she announced her definitive resolution to her husband, to Dorat, and to Boispille: "I ardently desire," said she to her husband, "to see myself again in France in a position to retrieve our fortunes, and to live tranquilly with you and my children, but I see so much danger in going there, as I understand affairs, that I cannot now risk it, knowing that I can neither work to your advantage nor theirs, if I am in trouble. I must therefore patiently seek some safe road which will finally carry me there with that repose of mind which I cannot now find. . . . I have heard of very important charges against me, of which I am positively innocent,—as perhaps they know at this moment,—and of which appearances indicate that they wish to accuse me. I cannot explain myself more clearly on this point." To the Abbé du Dorat, she said: "I am astonished that any one can accuse me of feigning imaginary apprehensions as an excuse for staying from the enjoyment of my lawful property, instead of pitying me for the perplexity to which my unhappy fortune reduces me." To Boispille, she said: "Since your departure, I have had so many new proofs of the continuance of my misfortunes in the suspicions which he entertains of me, that it is impossible for me to resolve to return and expose myself

[1] Letter of the Abbé du Dorat to Richelieu, *Manuscrits de Colbert* fol. 47.

to the consequences which may result from them. . . . Believe that I desire so ardently to return, that I would overlook many things to do so; but there are some that stop me with so much reason, that it is absolutely necessary that I should still remain where I am. I feel the inconveniences of this exile too deeply to refrain from ending them as soon as I can see light. Meanwhile, it is better to suffer than to perish."[1]

Thus vanished the last hopes of a sincere reconciliation between two persons who were at the same time attracted towards and repelled from each other by insurmountable instincts; who knew each other too well not to fear each other, or to confide in the promises of which neither was sparing without exacting binding pledges which neither could nor would be given. At Tours, two years before, Madame de Chevreuse had chosen rather to take for the second time the road to exile than to risk her liberty; at London, too, she preferred to endure the miseries of exile, and to consume the last days of her beauty in privation and fatigue if she might but remain free, with the hope of wearying fortune by the force of courage, and of making the author of her sufferings pay dearly for them.

In the middle of the year 1639, Marie de Medicis, weary of the wandering life that she was leading in the Netherlands at the mercy of the Spanish government, which had lavished promises on her in the hope of gaining her over to their party, and, on seeing her impotence, had then forsaken her, resolved to go to ask an asylum of her daughter, the Queen of England. Could the latter have refused this to her mother, aged, sick, and reduced to the last extremity? The pitiless Richelieu accuses Madame de Chevreuse[2] of having supported and seconded the resolution of Queen Henriette.

---

[1] *Manuscrits de Colbert*, fol. 53, etc.

[2] *Memoires*, vol. x., p. 484.

We should blame her if she had not done so, or if, herself exiled and unhappy, she had not mingled her respectful homage with that paid by the English Court to the widow of Henri IV., the mother of Louis XIII. and of three great queens, who had just braved a seven days' tempest on the ocean, and had arrived at last, destitute, despairing, and dying—a sad object for universal pity. Richelieu, who can see nothing but politics everywhere, pretends to find intrigues and plots in this homage as well as in the visits of Madame de Chevreuse to Marie de Medicis. These are probably the accusations of which Madame de Chevreuse complains in ambiguous language in her last letters. She repels them, and with reason—she remained tranquil, and was even very circumspect as long as she preserved the hope of a sincere reconciliation with Richelieu; but when sure that he sought to deceive her, to lure her to France to have her in his power, and, in case of need, to imprison her, having broken with him, she considered herself bound by no scruple, and only thought of giving him back war for war.

A little while after the arrival of Marie de Medicis, another victim of the cardinal, another exile, interesting at least for the incredible iniquity of the judgment rendered against him, came to London to seek a refuge. This was the Duke de La Valette, eldest son of the aged Duke d'Epernon and own brother of the Cardinal de La Valette, a general and confidant of Richelieu, whose daily counsels had often saved him from impostors, and whose sword had done good service for him in the Netherlands and in Italy. The Duke de La Valette had doubtless been guilty of a great fault. When placed under the command of M. le Prince at the siege of Fontarabie, he had caused the failure of this important enterprise by not seconding his general as he ought. He had not betrayed him, neither had he any understanding with the enemy, but a fatal jealousy of the Prince de Condé had made him fail in his duty. A just punishment would have satisfied the army;

the injustice of the trial and the excessive severity of the sentence aroused the indignation of all honorable men. Instead of being arraigned before the parliament in his quality of duke and peer, according to the laws of the time, Bernard de La Valette was delivered over to a commission as the Marshal de Marillac had formerly been. The duke fled, perceiving that they only sought his life, and they adjudged him guilty of contumacy in an unheard-of manner.[1] The king assembled in his chamber a certain number of the members of parliament, the chief justice, the *presidents à mortier*, a few counsellors of State, and several picked dukes and peers; of these he formed a sort of tribunal, placed himself at its head, presided himself, and, despite the generous resistance of the most of the members of parliament, who demanded that the affair should be referred to them in conformity with every ordinance, he forced these spurious judges to deliberate upon and to adopt the harsh conclusions of the attorney-general; and the Duke de La Valette was declared criminal of leze-majesty, and guilty of perfidy, treason, cowardice, and disobedience. He was condemned to be decapitated, his property confiscated, and his lands transferred from the united crown to the demesne of the king. The attorney-general, Mathieu Molé, extricated himself with difficulty from the duty of carrying this odious sentence into execution, and the illustrious criminal was beheaded in effigy upon the *Place de Grève* on the 8th of June, 1639. Such a method of procedure in a criminal case was a subversion of all the laws of the kingdom. If it dismayed magistrates attached to the king, and certainly not factious, like the presidents

---

[1] For this unheard-of scene, one should not only see the detailed and suspicious relation published by the friends of La Valette, which is found among the articles printed in the sequel of the *Memoires* of Montresor, but also the *Memoires* of Omer Talon, collection Petitot, ii. series, vol. lx., pp. 186–197.

Lejay, Novion, Bailleul, De Mesmes, and Bellièvre, is it surprising that it should have been revolting to the soul of a woman, and that Madame de Chevreuse should have entreated Charles I. to receive the noble fugitive into his kingdom? Mark well that the Duke de La Valette did not arrive in England until the end of October, 1639, when Madame de Chevreuse had no reason longer to preserve circumspection towards Richelieu. She interceded so earnestly with Charles I., that, despite the contrary opinion of the council of ministers, and thanks to the intervention of the queen, she obtained permission for the duke to reside in London, and even to be presented to the king, but secretly and private, so as not to offend France too greatly[1]—a vain precaution which did not save King Charles from the vindictive rancor of Richelieu. The cardinal, seeing that Madame de Chevreuse's influence with the King of England prevailed over his own, and that she urged him on to aid his enemies, more than ever endeavored to excite domestic troubles about the unhappy king which would put it out of his power to injure France, and covertly carried on his artful intrigues with the Parliamentarians, and most especially with the Scotch Puritans.[2] On her side, Madame de Chevreuse did not slumber. The ancient duel with Richelieu being once re-

---

[1] *Memoires* of Richelieu, vol. ii., pp. 498 and 499.

[2] See the letter of Richelieu to the Count d'Estrade of the 2d December, 1637; see also letters of Boispille to the cardinal of 1639, in which he gives the news of the slow progress of the army in Scotland with an ill-disguised satisfaction that betrays the sentiments of the writer. Richelieu caused the manifesto to England, which the Scotch published in 1641, to be printed in the *Gazette* of that year, No. 34, p. 161. "We cannot doubt," says the exact and learned Père Griffet, "that Richelieu was one of the prime movers of the revolution which finally led Charles I. to the scaffold and Oliver Cromwell to the throne. M. de Brienne seems to assent to this, but he takes care to remark that *things were carried much farther than the cardinal had foreseen or wished.*"

newed, she formed at London, with the Duke de Vendôme, La Vieuville, and La Valette, a faction of active and able exiles, who, supported by Count Holland, then one of the chiefs of the royalist party and of the army of Charles I., by Lord Montagu, a zealous Catholic and the confidential counsellor of Queen Henriette, by the Chevalier Digby and by other powerful lords of the English Court, and also maintaining direct correspondence with the Court of Rome through its English envoy, Rosetti,[1] as well as with the Cabinet of Madrid, encouraged and inflamed the hopes of the exiles and the malcontents, planted obstacles in the path of Richelieu, and gathered dangers everywhere about him.

In 1641, we find Madame de Chevreuse at Brussels serving as a bond between England, Spain, and Lorraine. The fact is not generally known, but we can demonstrate that she took an active part in the affair of the Count de Soissons; that is to say, in the most formidable conspiracy that had ever been plotted against Richelieu.

The Count de Soissons, prince of the blood-royal, was, however, of far more consequence than Henri de Montmorenci had been: he possessed his bravery and his military talents; his plan was better conceived, and the occasion more favorable in every respect. The prime minister, by straining all the springs of government, by perpetuating the war, by increasing the public taxes, and by oppressing both public and private individuals, had excited much hatred, and governed only by the force of terror. His genius was imposing, and the grandeur of his de-

[1] When afterwards, in 1643, the pope appointed the Cardinal Rosetti to represent him in the Congress at Munster, the successor of Richelieu unhesitatingly excluded him, founding this especially on the ground that, during his mission in England, Rosetti had been very intimate with Madame de Chevreuse, and that she had wholly gained him. Letter of the queen to M. de Fontenay, September 25, 1643. Bibliothèque Nationale, *fonds Gaignieres*, vol. 510, in fol., under the title: *Dépêsches importantes sur la paix d'Italie, des années* 1643 *et* 1644.

signs excited the admiration of a few choice spirits; but this continued harshness, joined with the sacrifices that were springing up unceasingly, wearied the greater number, and the king first of all. The favorite of the day, the Grand-Equerry Cinq-Mars, aspersed and undermined the cardinal as much as possible in the mind of Louis XIII. He knew of the conspiracy of the Count de Soissons, and favored, without taking part in it. They could count on him for the next day. Queen Anne, still in disgrace, despite the two sons which she had just given to France, would at least offer prayers for the end of a power which oppressed her. Monsieur had pledged his word—not very reliable, it is true; but the Duke de Bouillon, a warrior and an eminent politician, had openly declared himself; and his fortified town of Sedan, situated on the frontiers of France and Belgium, was an asylum in which they could brave for a long time all the forces of the cardinal. They had carefully arranged an extensive correspondence with every part of the kingdom, as well as with the clergy and the parliament. They even conspired in the Bastille, where the Marshal de Vitry and the Count de Cramail, prisoners as they were, had prepared a surprise with admirably guarded secrecy. The Abbé de Retz, then twenty-five years of age, preluded his adventurous career by this essay at civil war.[1] The Duke de Guise, who had escaped from the Archbishop of Rheims and taken shelter in the Netherlands, had promised to come to Sedan to share in the perils of the conspirators. But the greatest, the

[1] See the whole account of this affair in the first volume of the *Memoires*, p. 28–41. The author of the *Conjuration de Fiesque* attributes to himself on this occasion, some political discourses imitated from Sallust, in which maxims of state abound, according to that masculine style of the times of which Richelieu was the author and Corneille the interpreter. The discourses might have been added afterwards to give the reader an exalted idea of the precocious genius of Retz, but they are truthful, always excepting the usual charge, and accord perfectly with the most authentic documents.

most solid hope of the Count de Soissons, rested on Spain; she alone could enable him to depart from Sedan, to march against Paris, and to break the power of Richelieu; he therefore despatched one of the bravest and most intelligent of his followers to Brussels,[1] to negotiate with the Spanish ministers, and to obtain from them money and troops. This gentleman was named Alexandre de Campion. He met Madame de Chevreuse at Brussels, and confided to her the mission with which he was charged. She eagerly hastened to second it with all her influence. As we shall see this personage reappear more than once in the midst of the most tragic adventures in the life of Madame de Chevreuse, we must pause for a few moments to introduce him to our readers.

Indeed, he has taken care to draw his own portrait in a work entitled *Recueil de Lettres qui peuvent servir à l'histoire, et divers Poésies, à Rouen, aux dépens de l'auteur*, 1657. This work, designed but for a few persons and very little noticed at the time, and as little known since as though it had never existed, is, nevertheless, as the title asserts, very valuable to history. It is dedicated to the celebrated Gillonne d'Harcourt, Countess de Fiesque, one of the aides-de-camp of Mademoiselle during the war of the Fronde, a witty, intriguing, and brilliant woman. The book is pleasing. Alexandre de Campion there shows himself full of pretensions to wit and gallantry; he carefully collects all the little verses which he addressed in his youth to the belles of the time, and gives, without ceremony, the letters which he had formerly written under the most delicate circumstances, to the Count de Soissons,

---

[1] We read in the Gazette of Renaudot, for the year 1641, No. 61, p. 314: "The twentieth of this month of May, the Duke de Guise arrived at Brussels from Sedan, where he supped with the Duchess de Chevreuse and lodged at the house of Don Antonio Sarmiento." And in No. 64, p. 327, under the date of May 28: "The Secretary of the Duke de Bouillon has left here (Brussels) for Sedan, where the Duke de Guise has also returned."

the Duke de Vendôme, the Duke de Beaufort, the Count de Beaupuis, De Thou, the Duke de Bouillon, the Duke de Guise, Madame de Montbazon, and Madame de Chevreuse. We see in these letters that Alexandre de Campion, born in 1610, of a noble family of Normandy, in 1634 entered, at the age of twenty-four, into the service of the young Count de Soissons in the quality of gentleman, followed him in his different campaigns, distinguished himself therein, and gradually shared his confidence with Beauregard, Saint Ibar, and Varicarville—brave officers and men of honor, but restless and somewhat turbulent, who flattered the ambition of their master and urged him on in concert to play a conspicuous *rôle* in France by overthrowing the Cardinal de Richelieu. Campion informs us that, in the year 1636, the Count de Soissons began to meditate on what he afterwards executed, that he had a perfect understanding with the Duke de Bouillon, and that both exerted themselves to draw the Duke d'Orleans to Sedan, in order to raise there the standard of revolt, and constrain the king to sacrifice his minister. Campion went to Blois in order to secure the Duke d'Orleans and to point out to him the surest means of repairing to Sedan. At the same time, he was negotiating with Richelieu through Father Joseph. The close of the year 1636 and the whole of the year 1637 passed in these intrigues, which failed at last through the fear of trusting the conspirators to embark in the enterprise at the moment of action. The Count de Soissons ended by becoming reconciled with Richelieu through the medium of his brother-in-law, the Duke de Longueville, all the while preserving the intention of separating from the cardinal and of destroying him as soon as he should find a good opportunity. During this peace of short duration, the confidant of the Count de Soissons labored to procure himself partisans by every means. He connected himself with Cinq-Mars, and though the count was secretly engaged to a person whom he loved, and who is not named in the letters, Alexandre de Campion did not scruple to give several princesses and their families reason to hope for his hand. In 1640, the plot, which had never been entirely abandoned, was revived by the Duke de Bouillon and the Count de Soissons. The Grand-Equerry, without directly joining in it, promised his support.[1] Emanuel de Gondi, formerly general of the galleys, and now priest of the Oratory, father of the Duke de Retz and the future cardinal, and the Presidents de Mesmes and Bailleul were consulted, not as accomplices, but as friends. The penetrating Richelieu

---

[1] "August 20, 1640. M. le Grand is much pleased that I have added the compliments of M. de Bouillon to your own. He has charged me to offer you many in return, and especially to assure you that, at the proper time and place, you will see evidence that he was sincere in protesting to you, through me, that he was your most humble servant. He is certain that the cardinal designs to destroy him; from this you can judge of his intentions. He is on good terms with the queen, Monsieur, and yourself, and acts adroitly. No one knows that I see him, and if prosperity does not blind him, he is capable of undertaking something of importance. In any case, should you be pressed, and forced to take up arms to shield yourself from oppression, it is well to have for a protector near the king, an injured man, who, for his own interest, will not lose the occasion of destroying the one who wishes to ruin him. I know well that those who do not like him will chide his ingratitude because the Cardinal is his benefactor, but this does not concern you." Let us also transcribe this letter to De Thou of March 3, 1641, one year before the affair which led him to the scaffold: "I protest that neither the reasons which you alleged to me ten days since, in the Carmes-Déchaussés, nor those which you write me, persuade me in any manner, and that I have nothing to add to the answer I made you. A scheme like that in which you and your friend wish to embark me, which will at once be suspected by * * * who has no love for me, exposes me to his vengeance, and will end in nothing. I know the men, and their design of ruining him through the cabinet is a chimera which will destroy them and, perhaps, you also." There is another letter in the *Recueil* to De Thou, in which Alexandre de Campion informs him that he sends back a portrait, letters, and jewels, which his friend had confided to him, in order that he may return them "to that illustrious person for whom you are accused of sighing." Madame de Guymené is probably the person alluded to.

divined their purpose and removed them from the court and from Paris.[1] After remaining for some time on this perilous stage, where he often encountered the Abbé de Retz,[2] Campion was himself compelled to fly to Sedan. He was sent to Brussels to negotiate with Spain, and it was then that he became acquainted with Madame de Chevreuse. Did politics alone contribute to this liaison ? We know not, but when Alexandre de Campion recounts to the Count de Soissons all that he owes to Madame de Chevreuse, the gay young count rallies his young and chivalrous follower a little on his success with the beautiful duchess ; to which the latter replies with apparent modesty, mingled with considerable self-conceit : " June 3, 1641. M. de Chatillon (who commanded the army sent by Richelieu against the rebels) causes you but little fear, since you think of rallying me in your letter; and this is thanking me but little for the services which I render you in gaining an illustrious adherent to your party, and in procuring you a friend who otherwise would never have been such. She is persuaded of your friendship by the compliments which you offer her in your letters; but if she had seen what you have written to me, perhaps she would not act with so much zeal; your railleries not being over agreeable. She has written to the count-duke, so that you will have his assistance; and as she has entire power over Don Antonio Sarmiento, she has written to him also in the same strain; indeed, she is very zealous for you. I do not know that you would pay the debt as cheaply as you

[1] "December 24, 1640. According to your order, I shall show your letters to your mother, to the Père de Gondi, and to the Presidents de Mesmes and de Bailleul. . . But I shall take the liberty of telling you that I should be very glad to see them in private, lest the cardinal should know that they are your friends; it may ruin them if he discovers it." "January 1641. I do not doubt the displeasure which you have felt at the removal of the Père de Gondi and of the two presidents. I strongly suspect that their visits to the Hotel de Soissons were known."

[2] *Memoires*, vol. i., p. 26.

imagine if the state of your affairs should oblige you to make a tour hither, or if her own should compel her to take the road to Sedan; but if you will believe me, you will not have so flattering an opinion of me, since I constantly regard these superior deities with respect and veneration; and as they take care never to descend to me, I am careful never to raise my pretensions to them. Having spoken to you frankly, I venture to hope that you will both spare me for the future, and her who charges herself with advancing your affairs as if they were her own." But without ascribing to her more private reasons, Madame de Chevreuse was ready to serve with zeal in an enterprise directed against the common enemy. She wrote to the Count-Duke Olivares, and strongly enforced on him the demands of the Count de Soissons, and the Duke de Bouillon. At Brussels, she won over Don Antonio Sarmiento, and she gave to Campion, as well as to the Abbé de Merci, the intriguing agent in the service of Spain, letters to the Duke of Lorraine, in which she urged him not to lose this excellent occasion for repairing his past misfortunes, and for striking Richelieu a mortal blow. Charles IV., urged on at once by Madame de Chevreuse, by his relative, the Duke de Guise, by the Spanish minister, and, most of all, by his own restless and adventurous ambition, broke the solemn alliance which he had but recently contracted with France, entered into a treaty with Spain and with the Count de Soissons, and made haste to go to the aid of Sedan. General Lamboy and Colonel Metternich hastened from Flanders with six thousand imperialists, while, at the same time, Madame de Chevreuse and the exiles moved all the springs which were in their hands. France and Europe were in anxious expectation. Never had Richelieu been in greater danger; and the loss of the battle of the Marfée would have been fatal to him, had not the Count de Soissons met death in his triumph.

Did Madame de Chevreuse remain a stranger in 1642 to the new conspiracy of Monsieur, Cinq-Mars, and the Duke de

Bouillon? If so, it was the only one in which she was not concerned. It is very doubtful whether she was not in the secret, as well as Queen Anne, whose correspondence with Cinq-Mars and Monsieur cannot be contested. While conducting herself guardedly towards Louis XIII. and his minister, Anne of Austria had not abandoned her former sentiments nor even her designs, and she may even have been compromised in the affair of the Count de Soissons, if we may believe these notable words from Alexandre de Campion to Madame de Chevreuse, dated the 15th of August, 1641: "Have no fear of the letters which speak of *that person for whom of all others you have the greatest devotion;* M. de Bouillon and I have burned all which were in the count's casket." The queen certainly knew of the plot of Cinq-Mars and consented to it. Perhaps she was ignorant of the treaty with Spain, but in all else she acted in concert with the conspirators against the cardinal. La Rochefoucauld affirms this several times as a thing in which he had been concerned. "The eclat of the influence of M. le Grand," says he, "awakened the hopes of the malcontents: the queen and Monsieur joined themselves to him, and the Duke de Bouillon and several persons of rank followed their example. M. de Thou came to me on behalf of the queen to inform me of her alliance with M. le Grand, and to tell me that she had promised him that I would be among her friends."[1] The Duke de Bouillon[2] declares that the queen was firmly leagued with Monsieur and with the Grand-Equerry, and that she herself demanded his aid: "The queen, who had been persecuted by the cardinal in so many ways, doubted not that if the king should die, he would seek to take her children from her in order to procure for himself the regency?[3] She sought the Duke de Bouillon

[1] *Memoires*, ibid., pp. 362 and 363.

[2] *Memoires* of the Life of Fred. Maurice de la Tour d'Auvergne, Duke de Bouillon (by his secretary, Langlade), Paris, 1692, in 12mo.

[3] This fear was not without foundation, for Richelieu endeavored to

secretly through De Thou, and asked him whether, if the king should die, he would promise to receive her in Sedan, with her two children, believing that there would be no place of safety for them in all France, so much was she persuaded of the evil intentions of the cardinal and fearful of his power. De Thou said further to the Duke de Bouillon that, since the illness of the king, the queen and Monsieur, the Duke d'Orleans, were closely leagued together, and that it was through Cinq-Mars that this alliance had been made. Two days after, De Thou wished the queen to express to the Duke de Bouillon the satisfaction which she felt at the manner in which he had replied to what had been said to him in her behalf; this she could only do in a few words in passing, when going to the mass, committing the rest to De Thou as having entire confidence in him. Turenne, writing later to his sister, Mademoiselle de Bouillon, says to her: "You can judge how much it must affect my brother to see the queen and Monsieur still in power, while he has lost Sedan for the love of her."[1] Now, where Queen Anne was so deeply engaged, Madame de Chevreuse would scarcely have remained idle.

---

induce the king to grant him the guardianship of his children. He almost succeeded, as we see in this precious document, which we extract from the archives of foreign affairs, FRANCE, vol ci., letter of Chavigny to Richelieu of the 28th of July, 1642: "The king told me that several days since, at the time of his dangerous illness at the camp of Perpignan, M. le Grand endeavored in conversation to persuade him to give the guardianship of his children after his death to himself, without however saying it openly. Upon this, I took occasion to exaggerate the effrontery and horrible ambition of this profligate, and to show to his majesty that a person must have all the qualities which he had not in order to be capable of such guardianship, when he said to me, 'If God leaves me reason to direct what shall happen after my death, I can only leave them to Monseigneur the cardinal. To which I only replied by protestations on the part of his Eminence of affection and tenderness for so good a master.'"

[1] *Lettres et Memoires*, etc., published by General Grimoard in folio, vol. i., p. 40.

Let us add that she had long been very intimate with De Thou, who had been compromised on her account in some affair, the particulars of which it is impossible for us now to discover, but for which we know that he had great difficulty in obtaining his pardon from the cardinal, as he himself acknowledged in the fatal trial that brought him to the scaffold.[1] A friend of Richelieu, who does not reveal his name, but who seems to be well informed concerning the matter, does not hesitate to place Madame de Chevreuse as well as the queen among those who at that time sought to overthrow him. "M. le Grand," writes he to the cardinal, "has been urged on to his evil design by the queen-mother, her daughter, the queen of France, Madame de Chevreuse, and Lord Montagu, with other of the English papists." Lastly, the cardinal himself, who doubtless for his health, but also for his safety, had withdrawn to Tarascon in the beginning of June, 1642,[2] with his two confidants, Mazarin and Chavigny, and his faithful regiments of guards, feeling himself surrounded by perils, on representing to Louis XIII. the danger of his position, quotes what has been written him concerning Madame de Chevreuse as among its most striking indications.[3] Indeed, what party was it that was con-

---

[1] *Nouveaux Mémoires d'histoire, de critique et de littérature*, by the Abbé d'Artigny, vol. iv. *Pièces originales concernant le procès de MM. de Bouillon, Cinq-Mars et de Thou.* Examination of July 6, 1642, and more particularly the second examination of July 24. "Being questioned in respect to the affair of Madame de Chevreuse, he said that, having the word of the cardinal, he felt himself secure, well knowing that he would not grant pardon by halves."

[2] Archives of foreign affairs, FRANCE, vol. ci., letter of July 4.

[3] Archives of foreign affairs, FRANCE, vol. cii., inedited memoir of Richelieu. "It is necessary that MM. de Chavigny and De Noyers speak to the king and tell him that the cardinal, wishing to depart for Narbonne as he had advised for change of air, and not knowing what effect this might produce on his disease, wishes to express the entire confidence which he has in his majesty by informing him of the indications on every side. The letters of the Prince of Orange, the Gazette of Brus-

spiring against Richelieu? Was it not the party of former times, the party of the League of Austria and of Spain? And was not Madame de Chevreuse by her engagements with the Duke of Lorraine, the Queen of England, the Chevalier de Jars at Rome, and the Count-Duke Olivares at Madrid, made one of the chief powers of this party? When, therefore, it was seen to be in motion, it was very natural to suspect the hand of Madame de Chevreuse in all its movements.

But the eye of Richelieu soon pierced the darkness which enveloped it; he saw clearly into the intrigues of the Grand-Equerry whom he had long suspected, and a treason, the secret of which has remained impenetrable to all investigation for two centuries, threw into his hands the treaty that had been concluded with Spain, through the medium of Fontrailles, in the name of Monsieur, of Cinq-Mars, and of the Duke de Bouillon. Thenceforth the cardinal felt assured of victory. He understood Louis XIII.; he knew that he might, in a burst of his fitful and capricious temper, have complained to his favorite of his minister, and even have wished to be delivered from him, and thus have paved the way to dangerous conversation;[1] but he also knew to what degree he was a king and a Frenchman, and devoted to their common system of policy. He hastened, therefore, to send Chavigny to Narbonne with the authentic proofs of the Spanish treaty.

---

sels, and that of Cologne, the preparations of the queen-mother for leaving England, the litters and mules that have been purchased, all that has been written in genuine letters of Madame de Chevreuse, all that we hear from the courts of France, the rumors which are in the armies, the advices which come from the courts of Italy, the hopes of the Spaniards both on the side of Spain and Flanders, the resolution which Monsieur has taken of not coming as he had promised,—waiting, perhaps, for the result of the storm,—all these things oblige him to warn the king, in order that he may take such measures as he may please in respect to these rumors which disturb the public peace."

[1] See the *Memoires* of Monglat, Coll. Petitot, vol. i., p. 375.

At the sight of these proofs, Louis was troubled;[1] he could scarcely believe his own eyes, and he fell into a deep melancholy, from which he recovered with bursts of indignation against him who could thus abuse his confidence and conspire

[1] The details of this affair are not even given by the Père Griffet; they are only to be found in the archives of foreign affairs, FRANCE, vol. cii. During the first days of June, the domestic troubles of the king, the intrigues of Cinq-Mars, who was still at Narbonne, near him, and the dangers of the cardinal, were the subjects of Richelieu's inquiry, but not a word of the treaty of Spain. On the 12th of June all was made clear by the following billet of De Chavigny and De Noyers to Richelieu: "Narbonne, this 12th of June, at 10 A. M.—M. de Chavigny arrived this morning an hour before the king awakened. M. de Noyers and he, after having conferred together, sought his majesty, to whom they recounted in detail all the affairs of which he had been notified. All the measures have been taken in conformity with the views of his Eminence, and the despatches will be made this day without fail. The king approves of the journey of M. Castelan in Piedmont.—CHAVIGNY, DE NOYERS." Here all is clear. On the 11th of June Richelieu received the decisive news. He instantly sent Chavigny to the king with the proofs, and also with the measures he proposed to take. Chavigny travelled all night, and at twelve in the morning, in company with De Noyers, he saw the king, who read the despatches sent him by Richelieu, listened to the explanations of the ministers, and immediately approved and adopted the necessary measures, among which was the sending of Castelan to the Italian army to arrest the Duke de Bouillon. On the 12th Louis did not hesitate; but afterwards he fell a prey to gloomy reflections. Letter of De Noyers to Chavigny, who had returned to Tarascon, dated the 15th of June, says: "I think that it will be necessary to find means to enable M. de M. (azarin) to speak to the king, for strange thoughts trouble his mind. He said to me yesterday that he doubted whether one name had not been substituted for another. I thereupon said all that you can imagine to divert him from this idea, but he is still in a profound reverie. He was taken ill in the night, and at two took medicine, after which he slept for two hours. I saw him this morning, and gave him news of his Eminence, of whose improvement he was glad to hear. At the same time I showed him the extract from the letter of M. de Courbonne, and through this the arrangement of his Eminence with Savoy, and the advice concerning the islands. Upon this he made no comment, but said to

with a foreign power. There was no need of inflaming him; he was the first to demand an exemplary punishment; not a day, not an hour would he be moved by the youth of a culprit who had been so dear to him; he thought only of his crime, and signed his death-warrant without hesitation. If he spared the Duke de Bouillon, it was but in order to gain Sedan. He pardoned his brother, the Duke d'Orleans, but dishonored him and deprived him of all power in the State. Owing to a rumor proceeding from a servant of Fontrailles, and which the memoirs of Fontrailles fully confirm,[1] his suspicions rested on the queen,[2] and he could never be persuaded from the opinion that in this, as in the affair of Chalais, Anne of Austria was allied with Monsieur. What would he have said if he

---

me, "What a leap M. le Grand has made,' which he repeated two or three times." Another letter of the same date says: "I think that the sooner the Cardinal Mazarin comes here, the better it will be, for I perceive in truth that his majesty has need of consolation, and that his heart is very full." Letter of July 17th, De Noyers to Richelieu, concerning the arrangements of the king: "The king has said to us privately that Sedan is well worth an indemnity, but that he will never pardon M. le Grand, and that he will abandon him to the judges to act towards him according to their conscience." Letter of July 19th: "The king has entertained the thought of saving the life of M. de Bouillon in order to gain Sedan, but of leaving M. le Grand to his fate."

[1] *Relation de Fontrailles*, Coll. Petitot, vol. liv., p. 438: "When I was alone with M. de Thou (at Carcassonne, after the Spanish voyage) he suddenly spoke to me of the journey which I had just made, which surprised me greatly, as I thought it had been concealed from him. When I asked him how he had learned it, he frankly told me in confidence that he knew it from the queen, who had it from Monsieur. I admit that I did not think her so well informed, although I was not ignorant that her majesty had earnestly wished that a cabal might be formed in the court, and that she had contributed all in her power to it, as she could not but profit by it."

[2] Archives of foreign affairs, FRANCE, vol. cii. Chavigny to Richelieu, October 24: "The king gave the queen a bad reception yesterday. He is still greatly incensed against her, and constantly talks about it."

had read the relation of Fontrailles, the memoirs of the Duke de Bouillon, the note of Turenne, and the declaration of La Rochefoucauld? To our eyes, the accordance of these witnesses is decisive. The assertions of the Duke de Bouillon and of La Rochefoucauld are such that their authority can only be revoked by imputing to both, not an error merely, but a falsehood—and a falsehood at once gratuitous and odious. The queen used every effort to calm this new storm, and to persuade the king and Richelieu of her innocence. We have seen that in 1637 she did not hesitate to use the most solemn protestations and the most sacred oaths in the denial of that which she had afterwards been forced to confess. In 1642 she had recourse to the same means. She descended to humiliations as incompatible with a clear conscience as with her dignity and her rank. She lavished marks of attachment and interest on Richelieu; she affected a great horror of the ingratitude of the Grand-Equerry; she declared that she committed herself without reserve into the hands of the cardinal; that she only wished in future to be governed by his counsels, and that she would henceforth seek all her happiness in her children, whose education she abandoned to Richelieu. She wrote to him herself to inquire anxiously concerning his health, as she had formerly asked his hand and offered her own in token of eternal friendship, adding very humbly that he need not give himself the trouble of replying to her.[1]

---

[1] Archives of foreign affairs, ibid., vol. ci., letter of Le Gras, secretary of the queen's orders, to Chavigny. Saint Germain, July 2, 1642: "This extreme ingratitude is so shocking to her that she expresses her sentiments regarding it to the king in this letter, which she prays you to transmit to him." Ibid., vol. cii., letter of the Count de Brassac, superintendent of the queen's household, to Chavigny, dated July 20: "The queen cannot refrain from expressing the satisfaction which has driven away her indisposition, and which makes her seem so gay that every one sees plainly all that is in her heart." Ibid., vol. ci., another letter to Chavigny from Le Gras, in which he reminds him of his first

Anne went still further; she set no limits to her dissimulation and falsehood; in this extreme peril, she went so far as to turn against the courageous friend who had devoted herself for her. She would have embraced her as a liberator, had fortune declared itself in her favor; vanquished and disarmed, she abandoned her. As she had protested her horror of the conspiracy which had failed, and of her two imprudent and unfortunate accomplices, who mounted the scaffold without naming her, so, seeing the king and Richelieu incensed against Madame de Chevreuse, and determined to repulse the new attempts made by her family to obtain her recall, the queen, far from interceding for her former favorite, zealously joined with her enemies; and in order to mask her real sentiments, and to seem to applaud what she could not prevent, she asked as a special favor that the duchess should be kept far from herself and even from France. "The queen," writes Chavigny, the minister of foreign affairs, to Richelieu,[1] "the queen asked me if it were true that Madame de Chevreuse would return; then, without waiting for an answer, she said that she would be sorry to see her again in France, for she now understood her true character; and she commanded me to entreat his Eminence in her behalf, that, if he wished to do any thing for Madame de Chevreuse, it should be done without permitting

---

letter and that of M. de Brassac, etc. Ibid., Chavigny to Richelieu, July 28: "The queen is so grateful for the obligations that she owes to Monseigneur, that it would be difficult to change the resolutions which she has formed of acting in future only by the counsels of his Eminence, and of placing herself wholly in his hands. She commands me to give him this assurance on her part." Ibid., from the same to the same, Aug. 12: "I am persuaded that the friendship which the queen expresses for Monseigneur is without dissimulation, and that she will certainly continue it, asking no other favor than to be near her children, yet without pretending to govern them or to meddle with their education, which she earnestly desires Monseigneur to superintend. She has commanded me to assure his Eminence of this, and that she is extremely impatient to see him."

[1] Archives of foreign affairs, ibid. Letter of the 28th of July.

her return to France. I assured her Majesty that she should be satisfied on this point."—"I have never seen a truer or more sincere satisfaction than that which the queen felt on hearing what I said to her from Monseigneur. She protests that she not only does not wish Madame de Chevreuse to approach her, but that she is resolved, for her own safety, to suffer no person to advise her to the neglect of the most trifling part of her duty."[1]

Behold Madame de Chevreuse, then, fallen, as it seems, to the lowest depth of misfortune. Her situation was deplorable; she suffered in every chord of her heart; no hope remained to her of again seeing her country, her beautiful chateau, her children, her daughter Charlotte. Drawing almost nothing from France, she was at the end of resources, of loans, and of debts. She learned how hard it is *to mount and to descend the staircase of the stranger*;[2] to endure, by turns, the vanity of his promises and the haughtiness of his disdain. And that no bitterness might be spared her, the one who at least owed to her a silent fidelity, had openly ranged herself on the side of fortune and of Richelieu. She thus passed several most unhappy months, with no other support than her courage. Suddenly, on the 4th of December, 1642, the redoubted cardinal, victorious over all his enemies without and within, and absolute master of the king and the queen, succumbed while at the zenith of power. Louis XIII. was not long in following him; but, forced in spite of himself to confide the regency to the queen, and to appoint his brother lieutenant-general of the kingdom, he imposed on them a council, without whose consent they could do nothing, and in which should rule, in the capacity of prime minister, the man of all others the most devoted to the system of Richelieu, his particular friend, his confidant and his creature, the Cardinal Jules Mazarin. Even this capricious measure, which, through

[1] Ibid. Letter of August 12.

[2] Dante.

distrust of the future regent, placed royalty in some sort in commission, was not sufficient. Louis XIII. believed that he could only insure the tranquillity of his kingdom, after his death, by confirming and perpetuating, as far as was in his power, the exile of Madame de Chevreuse. In his pious aversion toward the active and enterprising duchess, he was accustomed to call her *le Diable.* He scarcely loved more, and he feared almost as much, the former keeper of the seals, Châteauneuf, who was imprisoned in the citadel of Angoulême. As if the shade of the cardinal still governed him on his death-bed, before expiring, he inscribed in his last will and testament, in the royal declaration of April 21, this extraordinary clause concerning Châteauneuf and Madame de Chevreuse: "Inasmuch, says the king, as for grave reasons, important to the good of our service, we have been obliged to deprive the Sieur de Châteauneuf of the office of Keeper of the Seals of France, and to cause him to be conducted to the citadel of Angoulême, where he has since remained by our orders, we will and require that the said Sieur de Châteauneuf shall remain in the same state in which he is at the present time in the said citadel of Angoulême, until after the peace shall be concluded and executed; with the proviso, however, that he shall not then be liberated except by the order of the Dame-Regent, together with the advice of the council, which shall prescribe a plan for his retreat either in the kingdom or out of the kingdom, as it shall deem best. And, as it is our design to provide against all the subjects who may in any manner disturb the judicious arrangement which we have made in order to preserve the repose and tranquillity of our state, the knowledge which we possess of the rebellious conduct of Madame de Chevreuse, of the artifices which she has used to excite dissension in our kingdom, and of the factions and the correspondence which she maintains abroad with our enemies, causes us to deem it proper to forbid her, as we do forbid her, the entrance to our kingdom during the war; willing, also, that after the peace shall be concluded and executed, she shall not return to our kingdom, except by the orders of the said Dame Queen Regent, together with the advice of the said council; with the additional proviso that she shall neither reside nor remain in any place near the court and the same Dame-Queen." These solemn words designated Madame de Chevreuse and Châteauneuf not only as the two most illustrious victims of the closing reign, but also as the chiefs of the new policy which seemed about to replace that of Richelieu. Louis XIII. breathed his last on the 14th of May, 1643. A few days after, the same parliament which had registered his testament amended it; the new regent was freed from all fetters and put in possession of the absolute sovereignty; Châteauneuf left his prison, and Madame de Chevreuse quitted Brussels in triumph to return to the court and to France.

SECOND PART.

Madame de Chevreuse and Mazarin.

CHAPTER III.

MAY, JUNE, AND JULY, 1643.

Madame de Chevreuse returns to the Court and to Paris.—New Arrangements of the Queen.—Anne of Austria and Mazarin.—Efforts of Madame de Chevreuse in favor of the former Party of the Queen and against the Policy and the Partisans of Richelieu.—Her Solicitations in behalf of Châteauneuf, the Vendômes, and La Rochefoucauld.—Her Home and Foreign Policy.—Madame de Chevreuse the true Chief of the Party of the Importants.—Defeated in her efforts to gain the Queen, she resolves to have recourse to other means.—A Crisis becomes inevitable; it occurs on the occasion of the Quarrel between Madame de Montbazon and Madame de Longueville.

On the 20th of June, 1643, the following article appeared in Renaudot's *Gazette*, the *Moniteur* of the times:[1]

Their Majesties having despatched the Sieur de Boispille, steward of the household of the Duke de Chevreuse, to Brussels, to hasten the return of his wife, the duchess, she set out from there on the 6th of this month, accompanied by twenty carriages filled with the noblest lords and ladies of that court, who escorted her as far as Notre Dame de Hau. The next day she reached Mons in Hainault, passing through the Spanish army that lies encamped in the valley, where she lodged, and thence by Condé arrived on the 9th at Cambrai, being everywhere honorably received by the governors and the no-

[1] No. 77, p. 519.

bles of the country, and escorted by them a league beyond the said Cambrai, where the Sieur d'Hocquincourt[1] received her on the French frontier, and, conducting her to Peronne, of which he was governor, gave her there a magnificent reception. She was visited there by the Duchess de Chaulne, and on the 12th was conducted thence by the Duke de Chaulne[2] to his house, where she was splendidly entertained. Leaving Chaulne the same day, she reached Roye, where she lodged, and on the 13th arrived at Versine, the house of the Sieur de Saint Simon, brother of the duke of the same name, where the Duke de Chevreuse was awaiting her, and where she was received and treated in the same manner. Finally, on the 14th of this month, she reached Paris, ten years after having quitted it; in which absence this princess has shown what a brave spirit like her own can do, despite the strokes of adverse fortune which her constancy has surmounted. She went instantly to salute their majesties, in which visit she received so many tokens of the queen's affection, and gave to her so many proofs of zeal in every thing that related to her interests, and also of entire resignation to her will, that it seems most evident that neither absence, nor distance, nor the cares of business, can effect any change in any but vulgar souls. But the great retinue of court nobles who visit her continually, and fill her spacious palace to overflowing,[3] does not inspire one with so much ad-

---

[1] The future Marshal d'Hocquincourt, a warrior and pleasure-lover, and a fickle politician, who, in the Fronde, strayed from Mazarin to Condé, and wrote to Madame de Montbazon, *Peronne est à la belle des belles.*

[2] The Duke and Marshal de Chaulne was the second brother of the Constable de Luynes.

[3] Not the Hôtel de Luynes, the residence of the son of the constable, on the Quai des Grands-Augustins, at the corner of the Rue Git-le-cœur, of which Perelle has executed a charming little engraving, and in which the Chancellor Séguier took refuge during the Fronde, when the populace attacked him on the Pont-Neuf when going to the parliament, but

miration as does the fact that neither the fatigues of her long journeys, nor the ills of her rigorous fortune, have wrought any change in her natural magnanimity, nor, which is still more extraordinary, in her beauty.

Behold the seeming!—see now the reality. Madame de Chevreuse was then forty-three years of age. Her beauty, which had been tried by so many fatigues, was still surviving, but was beginning to decline. Her love for admiration still existed, but in a weaker degree, while her taste for politics took the lead. She had seen the most celebrated statesmen in Europe; she knew almost all the courts, with the strength and the weakness of the different governments, and she had gained in her journeyings a vast experience. She hoped to find Queen Anne such as she had left her, disliking business and very willing to let herself be guided by those for whom she had a particular affection; and as Madame de Chevreuse believed herself the first affection of the queen, she thought to exercise over her the two-fold ascendency of friendship and of talent. More ambitious for her friends than for herself, she saw them already recompensed for their long sacrifices, everywhere replacing the creatures of Richelieu, and at their head as prime minister, him for whom she had separated herself from the triumphant cardinal and had endured an imprisonment of ten years. She did not attach much importance to Mazarin, whom she did not know, whom she had never seen,

---

the Hôtel de Chevreuse, Rue Saint-Thomas du Louvre, next the Hôtel Rambouillet, a magnificent palace, built by the Marquis de Vieuville while he was superintendent of finances, and purchased in 1620 by the Constable de Luynes, and which, after his death and the new marriage of his widow, was called the Hôtel de Chevreuse, becoming afterwards the Hôtel d'Epernon, and still later, in 1663, the Hôtel de Longueville. Madame de Chevreuse then caused the beautiful palace of the Rue Saint-Dominique-Saint-Germain to be built by the celebrated artist Lemuet. This has also been represented by Perelle, and is now occupied by the Duke de Luynes.

and who seemed to her without support at the court and in France, while on the contrary she felt herself sustained by all its rank, its power, and its credit. She believed herself sure of Monsieur, who could easily rule his wife, the beautiful Marguerite, sister of Charles IV. Having just returned from Flanders, she could dispose of nearly all of the house of Rohan and of the house of Lorraine, particularly of the Duke de Guise and the Duke d'Elbeuf. She could count on the Vendômes, on the Duke d'Epernon, and on La Vieuville, her former companions of exile in England; on the Bouillons, if maltreated; on La Rochefoucauld, whose spirit and pretensions were known to her; on Lord Montagu, who had been her admirer, and who then possessed the entire confidence of Anne of Austria; on La Châtre, the friend of the Vendômes and colonel-general of the Swiss, on Tréville, on Beringhen, on Jars, on La Porte, and on many others who had lately quitted prison, exile, and disgrace. Among the women, her mother and sister-in-law, Madame de Montbazon and Madame de Guymené, the two great beauties of the day, who drew after them a numerous train of old and new admirers, seemed to her already gained. She knew, too, that one of the first acts of the new regent had been to recall near her person two noble victims of Richelieu, Madame de Senecé and Madame de Hautefort, whose piety and virtue would usefully conspire with other influences to give them a valuable support in the conscience of Anne of Austria. All these calculations seemed certain, all these hopes well founded, and Madame de Chevreuse quitted Brussels in the firm persuasion that she was about to enter the Louvre in triumph. She was mistaken; the queen was changed, or very nearly so.

If the time has come for restoring Louis XIII. to the place in history that belongs to him, it is also time to do justice to Anne of Austria. She was no ordinary person. Beautiful and needing to be loved, and at the same time vain and haughty, she had been deeply wounded by the coldness and neglect of her husband, and, in a spirit of vengeance as well as of coquetry, she had amused herself by exciting more than one passion in those about her, but without ever overstepping the limits of Spanish gallantry. She had submitted with impatience to be treated contemptuously, deprived of all power, and held in a sort of permanent disgrace by the king and Richelieu; but this aroused in her heart a subdued yet bitter opposition to the government of the cardinal. She had even been engaged in various enterprises which, as we have seen, had been unsuccessful and had involved her in great danger. She then called to her aid another of her womanly and Spanish talents, dissimulation. Misfortune speedily taught her this "ugly, but necessary virtue," as Madame de Motteville calls it,[1] and we have seen that she made rapid progress in it. Naturally indolent, she had no love for business; yet she was sensible and even courageous, and capable of understanding and of following counsel. Hitherto she had played a double game; striving to make to herself partisans in secret, to encourage and urge forward the malcontents, to endeavor to escape from the yoke of the cardinal, and notwithstanding, to look pleasantly on him, to lull him by false demonstrations, to humiliate herself when necessary, to gain time—and to wait. After the death of Richelieu, feeling herself stronger both by her two children and by the incurable malady of Louis XIII., she had but a single aim to which she sacrificed every thing—that of being regent—and she succeeded in this, thanks to a rare patience, to infinite caution, and to an adroit and well-sustained course of conduct; thanks also to the unhoped-for service rendered her by Mazarin, the principal minister of the king. Anne neglected nothing in order to subdue the king's resentment; she unceasingly lavished on him the tenderest cares, passing both days and nights by his side; she protested with tears that she had never failed in her duty to him, that

---

[1] Vol. i., p. 186.

she was a stranger to the plot of Chalais, and that all the accusations which had been heaped upon her were without foundation. All this had but little effect on the mind of the king, who contented himself with saying:[1] "In my present state, it is my duty to forgive her, but I am not obliged to believe her." He had always suspected her of being in correspondence with Spain and under the sway of Madame de Chevreuse, and he wished to exclude her from the regency, as well as his brother, the Duke d'Orleans, whom he neither loved nor respected. Mazarin had great difficulty in making him comprehend that it was impossible to deprive the queen of the title of regent, and that all that could be done was to take from her all power, by the appointment of a carefully arranged council whose advice she would be obliged to follow by acting in conformity with the voice of the majority. Anne submitted to these hard and humiliating conditions without a murmur; she acknowledged the royal declaration of the 21st of April, which restricted her authority within the narrowest limits, and perpetuated the exile of Châteauneuf and of Madame de Chevreuse; and signed it, pledging herself to maintain it. After all, she was in possession of the regency; and as she owed this to the same scheme which limited her power, far from being displeased with its author, she regarded it as a first service which merited some acknowledgment. Observe a fact which most historians have overlooked, but which has not escaped the penetration of La Rochefoucauld, who mingled in all the intrigues of the day: "The Cardinal Mazarin," says he, "justified in some sort this harsh declaration; he represented it as an important service rendered to the queen, it being the only means which could persuade the king to consent to the regency. He showed her that it mattered little to her on what conditions she had received it, provided it was with the consent of the king, and that means would not be

---

[1] La Rochefoucauld, *Memoires*, p. 369.

wanting eventually for strengthening her power and enabling her to govern alone. These reasons, which were supported somewhat by appearances and urged with all the art of the cardinal, were the more readily accepted by the queen, that he who advanced them was beginning to be not altogether disagreeable to her."

Mazarin, in truth, had had no share in the annoyances which the queen had endured; she had therefore no reason for disliking him except that he had been one of the intimate friends of Richelieu; but he had none of the disagreeable airs of the cardinal, he had taken part in the recall of the exiles, and had shielded the queen's regency from the suspicions of the king. His ability was proved, and Anne with her indolence and inexperience, in the beginning of a reign beset on every side from without and within with the greatest difficulties, had need of some one who would leave to her the honor of supreme authority while he took upon himself the weight of affairs; and she saw no one among her friends whose capacity was sufficiently tried to inspire her with confidence. She appreciated the talents and address of La Rochefoucauld, but she could not think of so young a minister. The two men nearest her, the Duke de Beaufort, youngest son of the Duke de Vendôme, and her grand almoner, Potier, Bishop of Beauvais, were devoted servants for whom she intended to do much at some future day, but whom she dared not yet intrust with the government. To wait a little, therefore, seemed the wisest course to her. Mazarin had more than one secret interview with her. He showed himself zealous to serve her, and not unwilling to sacrifice to her some of the former ministers of Richelieu who had displeased her most, and to act in concert with those of her friends to whom she deemed herself under indispensable obligations. He had the art to put himself on good terms with the Bishop of Beauvais, the spiritual director of the queen. He deceived him, as he deceived the Duke de Beaufort and all the rest, by affecting great disinterestedness, and by pretending to be on the point of going to enjoy the privileges and honors of the cardinalate at Rome, in the bosom of his family and the home of the arts.[1]

Lastly, there is a delicate point which La Rochefoucauld scarcely touches, but which history cannot leave in the shade without ignoring the cause which first gave power to Mazarin, and soon became the knot and the key of his position—Anne of Austria was a woman, and Mazarin did not displease her. To quote our own words in another work,[2] "After having been so long oppressed, the royal authority delighted Anne of Austria, and her Spanish soul craved respect and homage. Mazarin lavished them upon her. He threw himself at her feet in order to reach her heart. In her heart she was scarcely affected by the grave accusation which was already raised against him—that he was a foreigner—for she was also a foreigner; perhaps, indeed, this was a secret attraction to her, and she found a peculiar charm in conversing with her prime minister in her mother-tongue as with a fellow-countryman and a friend. Add to all this the mind and the manners of Mazarin; he was pliant and insinuating; always master of himself, of an immovable serenity in the gravest emergencies, full of confidence in his good star, and diffusing his confidence everywhere about him. It must also be said that—cardinal as he was—Mazarin was not a priest; that, nourished in the maxims of the gallantry of her country, Anne of Austria had always loved to please; that she was forty-one years of age and was still beautiful; that her minister was of the same age, and that he was well-made, with a pleasing face, in which refinement was joined with dignity. He had quickly perceived that without family, without establishment, and without support in France, surrounded by rivals and by enemies, all his power was in the

---

[1] See the beginning of Mazarin, La Rochefoucauld, Madame de Motteville, La Châtre, and both the Briennes.

[2] *La jeunesse de Madame de Longueville*, 3d edit., ch. iii., p. 217.

queen. He therefore endeavored first of all to reach her heart, as Richelieu before him had attempted; but he possessed many more means of succeeding; and the handsome and pleasing cardinal *did* succeed. Once master of her heart, he easily guided the mind of Anne of Austria, and taught her the difficult art of always pursuing the same end under the most varied guises, according to the diversity of circumstances."

But how much time and pains were needed for Mazarin to bring Anne of Austria to this point, and to triumph over all her scruples! The history of the progress of Mazarin in the heart of the queen is the true history of the first three months of the regency. Anne commenced on the 18th of May, 1643, by easily persuading herself to retain, for a time at least, the minister whom Louis XIII. had bequeathed and commended to her. We shall see to what point she had arrived on the 2d of September of the same year.

It was impossible for her to preserve the order of the royal declaration which established Mazarin as prime minister and presiding officer of the council under the Prince, since she wished to have all this part of the testament of the late king broken by the parliament as limiting the authority of the regent, contrary to all usages. It was therefore agreed in preliminary cabals that Mazarin should renounce the sort of right which the royal declaration gave him, but that at the same time, the regent, freed from all fetters, should voluntarily offer him a similar place, so that he would hold his power, not from the will of the deceased king, but from the free gift of the queen. All this was concluded between them with such secrecy that the surprise was great and general when, on the 18th of May, the parliament was seen to invest the regent with the sovereign authority, while on the same day the Cardinal Mazarin was placed at the head of the cabinet. This was the result of a skilfully contrived plot which the queen had concealed from all her friends who were opposed to Mazarin.

And from this day, too, the cardinal could perceive that he had found in Queen Anne, in respect to dissimulation and diplomatic conduct, a pupil worthy of himself, and already far advanced in her studies.

Mazarin soon established himself in the favor of Anne of Austria by his double talent as a laborious and indefatigable statesman and as a finished courtier. He took all the cares of government upon himself, while he never hesitated to yield her all the honors of success. He employed wonderful skill and assiduity in instructing without ever wounding her. His great art was to persuade her that he only wished for power in order to serve her better; that, a foreigner, without family and without friends, he depended entirely on her and wished to draw his support from her alone. Such language, supported by ability of the first order, could not fail to please, and it can be said with truth that the widow of Louis XIII. had already another Richelieu near her in the beginning of June, 1643, when Madame de Chevreuse quitted Brussels.

The disciple and the confidant of Richelieu and Louis XIII., Mazarin had inherited their opinions and their feelings concerning Madame de Chevreuse. He understood her although he had never seen her, and he profoundly distrusted her as well as her friend Châteauneuf. A favorite of such talents and of such a character, full of persuasion and of courage, an open advocate for peace, and secretly attached to the Duke of Lorraine, to Austria, and to Spain, who had at her beck an ambitious and capable man, was utterly incompatible with the favor to which he aspired, and with all his diplomatic and warlike designs. He felt that there was not room enough for both in the heart of Anne of Austria, and he prepared to combat her in his own manner, stealthily and by degrees as occasions might offer.

Mazarin possessed a secret and powerful ally against Madame de Chevreuse in the new and growing taste of the queen for repose and for a tranquil life. She had formerly been somewhat restless because she had been oppressed; now, having attained the supreme power, and happy in the beginning of a new attachment, she dreaded troubles and adventures, and feared Madame de Chevreuse almost as much as she loved her. The artful cardinal studied to nourish this disquietude. He was supported by the Princess de Condé, then high in favor with the queen by reason of her own merit, by that of her husband, M. le Prince, by the brilliant exploits of her son, the Duke d'Enghien, by the services of her son-in-law, the Duke de Longueville, who had honorably commanded the armies in Italy and Spain, and by the virtues of her daughter, Madame de Longueville, but lately married and already the delight of the salons and the court. Madame the Princess, Charlotte-Marguerite de Montmorenci, formerly so celebrated for her beauty, had also, at one time, loved homage like Queen Anne; but, although still beautiful, she had now become grave and zealously religious. She disliked Madame de Chevreuse, and she detested Châteauneuf, who, in 1632, had presided at Toulouse at the judgment and condemnation of her brother Henri. She labored, therefore, in concert with Mazarin, to destroy or at least to weaken Madame de Chevreuse with the queen. They were armed with the last will of Louis XIII., and nearly succeeded in raising a scruple in the queen as to violating it so speedily. They urged that days once gone by could never return, that the amusements and the passions of early youth were "bad accompaniments[1] of a riper

---

[1] These are the exact words of Madame de Motteville, vol. i., p. 162. This passage is so important that we must give it here entire: "Many visits and compliments were made to Madame de Chevreuse as to one who had once reigned in the heart of the queen, and who, in all her disgrace, had always maintained a correspondence with her and had seemed to possess her entire friendship. To this might be added the obligations of her sufferings, which had led her over all Europe; and although her travels might have tended to her glory, and have given her the means of triumphing over a thousand hearts, in respect to the queen they were

age," that before all else she was a mother and a queen, that Madame de Chevreuse, passionate and frivolous as she was, no longer suited her, that she had never brought happiness to any one, and that by loading her with riches and honors, she would sufficiently acquit herself of her debt of gratitude.

To do honor to her old friend, the queen sent La Rochefoucauld to meet her, but charged him to inform her of the new arrangements which she would find on her return. La Rochefoucauld had an earnest conversation with Anne of Austria, in which he did every thing to win her back to Madame de Chevreuse: "I spoke to her," says he, "perhaps, more freely than I ought. I placed before her eyes the fidelity of Madame de Chevreuse, her long services, and the harshness of the

---

chains which should have bound her more strongly than in the past. But the affairs of this world cannot always remain in the same state, and this change natural to mankind caused Madame de Chevreuse, who was distrusted and vilified by those aspiring to the ministry, to find the queen changed in her absence, while this same change also caused the queen to find the duchess wanting in the charms which had formerly fascinated her. The sovereign had become more thoughtful and religious, while the favorite still retained her former tastes for gallantry and frivolity, which were bad accompaniments of a riper age. Her rivals had assured the queen that she wished to rule her, and the queen was so strongly impressed with this fear that, considering the prohibition of it which the king had made, she had some difficulty in resolving on the speedy return of the duchess; this indeed was laudable in the queen, and should be respected. Madame the Princess, who hated Madame de Chevreuse, and whose tastes were similar to those of the queen, had used every effort in her power to disgust her with her former favorite. Absence had in some measure served to weaken the duchess' hold upon the mind of the queen, while her presence had contributed much to her friendship with, or rather to accustom her to, Madame the Princess. However, when the distinguished exile arrived, the queen seemed rejoiced to see her, and treated her with favor. I had returned to the court a few days before. As soon as I had the honor of approaching the queen, I saw what were her sentiments towards Madame de Chevreuse, and I knew that the new minister had exerted himself as much as possible to show her her faults."

misfortunes which she had drawn upon herself. I entreated her to consider of what fickleness she would be thought capable, and what interpretation would be given to this fickleness, should she prefer Cardinal Mazarin to Madame de Chevreuse. This conversation was long and stormy; I saw clearly that I had incensed her."[1] However, he went to meet the duchess on the road to Brussels, and encountered her at Roye. Montagu had preceded him. La Rochefoucauld came in the name of the queen; Montagu in the name of Mazarin. This was no longer the brilliant Montagu, the friend of Holland and of Buckingham and the impassioned cavalier of Madame de Chevreuse, age had changed him also; he had turned devotee, and he entered the church a few years after. He still remained attached to the object of his former adoration; but before all else, he belonged to the queen, and consequently, to the interests of Mazarin.[2]

He came to place the homage of the prime minister at the feet of Madame de Chevreuse, and to strive to ally the old and the new favorites. La Rochefoucauld, always eager to assume a prominent character together with the air of a great politician, asserts that he "entreated Madame de Chevreuse not to attempt to rule the queen at first, but simply to endeavor to regain the place in her heart and affections of which she had been deprived, and to place herself in a position some day to protect or to destroy the cardinal, according to circumstances and his future course of conduct." Madame de Chevreuse wished also to hear the counsels of another of her friends—less illustrious but more devoted—that Alexandre de Campion, whom she had known two years before at Brussels, and who,

[1] *Memoires*, ibid., p. 378.

[2] He had been on the side of Mazarin in the cabals which preceded the regency, and we find in the archives of foreign affairs, FRANCE, civ., the fragment of a letter from Montagu to the queen, without date, but written about this time, in which he pledges himself in a mystic language to turn a deaf ear to malcontents, and to remain attached to her ministry.

after the death of the Count de Soissons, had entered the service of the Vendômes, together with his brother Henri, an officer of tried courage. She invited Alexandre de Campion to come to meet her at Peronne, and he seems to have given her the same counsel as La Rochefoucauld, if we may judge from the note which he wrote to her at the end of May, before quitting Paris to rejoin her:[1] "I do not know," says he, "what M. Montagu may negotiate with you, but I am certain that he will offer you money on the part of Cardinal Mazarin to pay your debts, and also that he has held out hopes to him of forming a firm friendship between you and him. I do not believe that he will find you strongly disposed to make this alliance, both because your best friends in France are not on very good terms with him, and because he seems leagued with the friends of the late cardinal. For my part, the counsel which I take the liberty of giving you on this subject is, that you do not take any decided resolution until you shall have seen the queen, by whose sentiments you will no doubt gladly shape your course, both on account of the zeal which you have for her and the friendship which she entertains for you. I am sure from my knowledge of your character that I shall have more trouble in holding you back than in urging you on, seeing the friendship which you have done me the honor to confess to me for a certain person, (evidently Châteauneuf;) but apart from this consideration and that of many other honorable men embarked in the same cause, I do not see the necessity of perpetuating a hatred so far as even to carry it beyond the death of our enemies. I have no love for the cardinal, but I wish no harm to any of his race. After all, Madame, all that I can write is not the twentieth part of what I have to say to you; and I dare assure you that at Peronne you will be as well informed of the prevailing feeling as if you were in Paris." Madame de Chevreuse listened to the counsels of her

[1] *Recueil*, etc.

three friends and promised to follow them—and in fact, she did follow them, but in conformity with her character and with the interests of the party whom she had long served and would not now abandon. As the queen showed much joy at seeing her again, she did not at once perceive the change which had taken place in her feelings, and she persuaded herself that her constant presence would soon restore to her her former empire.

The first thing that Madame de Chevreuse proposed was the return of Châteauneuf. La Rochefoucauld gives us here a portrait of the ex-keeper of the seals, somewhat flattering perhaps, but not at all exaggerated, in which he imperfectly discloses the plan of the government which his friends, the Importants, wished to give to France—the same which the earliest Frondeurs afterwards acknowledged, and still later, the friends of the Duke de Bourgogne, the last Importants of the seventeenth century: "The good sense and the long political experience of M. de Châteauneuf," says La Rochefoucauld,[1] "were well known to the queen. He had endured a rigorous imprisonment for having been in her interest; he was firm, decisive, attached to the State, and more capable than any other in France of re-establishing the ancient system of government which Cardinal de Richelieu had begun to destroy. He was, besides, intimately attached to Madame de Chevreuse, and she well knew the surest methods of ruling him. She therefore urged his return with many entreaties." Châteauneuf had already obtained permission to exchange the gloomy prison where he had pined for ten years for a sort of exile on one of his estates.[2] Madame de Chevreuse demanded the end

---

[1] Ibid., p. 380.

[2] Archives of foreign affairs, FRANCE, vol. c., p. 135. Autograph letter of Châteauneuf to Chavigny, March 23, 1643, during the lifetime of Louis XIII., in which he "thanks him for the assistance which he has lent his sister, Madame de Vaucelas, in attempting to release him from the rude and miserable condition in which he has been confined for ten

of even this modified exile, and that she might again see him who had suffered so deeply for the queen and for herself. Mazarin perceived that it was necessary to grant this, but he yielded slowly, without seeming of himself to repulse Châteauneuf, yet urging the necessity of managing the Condés, especially Madame the Princess, who, as we have already said, hated him as the judge of Henri de Montmorenci. Châteauneuf was therefore recalled, but with this reserve, professedly accorded to the last wishes of the king, that he should not appear at court, but remain at his estate of Montrouge, near Paris, where his friends could visit him.

The question was how to transfer him thence to the ministry. Châteauneuf was old, it is true, but neither his energy nor his ambition had abandoned him, and Madame de Chevreuse regarded it as a debt of honor which she owed him to replace him in the office of keeper of the seals, which he had formerly filled and had lost for her sake, and which all the former friends of the queen saw with indignation in the hands of one of the most servile of the creatures of Richelieu, Pierre Séguier. Séguier was a very capable man, laborious, well-informed, full of resources, and with no character of his own, whose suppleness, joined with his ability, rendered him a convenient and useful tool for a prime minister. His conduct in the trial of De Thou had made him odious. He had forced Monsieur to submit to an interrogation in this same affair;

---

years, at an advanced age, and full of maladies which have constantly tormented him." He was not released until the commencement of the regency. Ibid., p. 404: "Angoulesme, May 25, 1643. Sire, I render most humble thanks to your Majesty for the favor which she has been pleased to grant me after so long a detention, in permitting me to retire to one of my estates. The few days which remain to me shall be spent in praying to God for your Majesty that he may be pleased to grant her many years of happiness. These most devout supplications, Sire, are made for your Majesty by your most humble and obedient subject and servant, Châteauneuf."

and previous to this in the affair of 1637, he had not respected the asylum of the queen at the Val-de-Grace. He had enriched himself, and his fortune had procured illustrious alliances for his daughters. An outcry was raised against him, and his dismissal was demanded from every side. Two things saved him. First, his successor could not be agreed upon. Châteauneuf was the candidate of the Importants and of Madame de Chevreuse, but President Bailleul, the superintendent of the finances, coveted the place for himself, the Bishop de Beauvais feared such a colleague in the cabinet as Châteauneuf, and the Condés opposed him. Then Séguier had a sister who was very dear to the queen, the Mother Jeanne, superior of the convent of the Carmelites of Pontoise. The virtues of the sister pleaded in favor of the brother, and Montagu, who was wholly devoted to the Mother Jeanne, warmly defended the keeper of the seals.

Madame de Chevreuse, perceiving that it was almost impossible to surmount so strong an opposition, took another road whereby to arrive at the same end; she contented herself with asking the smallest place in the cabinet for her friend, knowing that once there, Châteauneuf would know how to accomplish the rest, and to elevate his position. President Bailleul, superintendent of the finances, having shown an inferior capacity for this place, it became necessary to give him a new assistant when the Count d'Avaux, with whom he shared the duties of the office, went to Munster.[1] Madame de Chevreuse insinuated to the queen that she could easily introduce Châteauneuf into the council by appointing him the successor of D'Avaux, a modest position which could not excite the distrust of Mazarin; but the latter understood the manœuvre and baffled it. He easily persuaded the queen to

[1] Carnet's *Autographes de Mazarin*, preserved at the *Bibliothèque Nationale*, ii. Carnet, p. 16. *Non faccia sua Maestà sopraintendente Chatonof, se non vuol, restabilirlo intieramente.*

sustain Bailleul, who was chancellor of her household, and for whom she had a regard, by placing near him as controller-general the able D'Hemery, who afterwards superseded him. At the same time that she was thus laboring to extricate from disgrace the man on whom all her political hopes depended, Madame de Chevreuse, not daring to attack Mazarin openly, insensibly mined the earth about him and prepared his ruin. Her practised eye enabled her easily to recognize the most favorable point of attack in the assault which was to gain the surrender of the queen, and the watchword which she gave was to maintain and to heighten the general feeling of reprobation which all the exiles, on returning to France, had excited and diffused against the memory of Richelieu. This feeling existed everywhere,—in the noble families, decimated or despoiled, in the Church, too sternly ruled not to be cruelly oppressed, in the parliaments, reduced to a mere judiciary body above which they very much aspired—it was still living in the heart of the queen, who could not forget the deep humiliation to which she had been subjected by Richelieu, and the fate which he had probably held in store for her. These tactics succeeded; a tempest rose on every side against violence and tyranny, and consequently, against the creatures of Richelieu, which Mazarin had much trouble in abating.[1]

Madame de Chevreuse then entreated the queen to repair the long misfortunes of the Vendômes by giving them either the admiralty, to which immense power was attached, or the government of Brittany, which the head of the family, César de Vendôme, had formerly possessed, and which he held by the authority of his father, Henri IV., and by inheritance from his step-father, the Duke de Mercoeur. This was at once demanding the restoration of a friendly house, and the

---

[1] See *La Jeunesse de Madame de Longueville*, chap. iii., p. 216: the letter written by Mazarin concerning this to the Duke de Brézé, May 28, 1643.

ruin of the two families which had most served Richelieu, and could best sustain Mazarin. The Marshal de La Meilleraie, grand master of the artillery, and recently invested with the government of Brittany, was a warrior of authority, and in possession of several regiments. The Duke Maillé de Brézé, step-brother of Richelieu, was also a marshal, and governor of the important province of Anjou; and his son, Armand de Brézé, then at the head of the admiralty, passed already, despite his youth, for the first sailor of his time. Mazarin warded off the blow aimed at him by the duchess by force of address and patience; never refusing, always eluding, and calling to his aid his great ally, as he styled it, Time. Before the return of Madame de Chevreuse, he had himself endeavored to gain the Vendômes, and to attach them to his interest. At the death of Richelieu, he had contributed much to their recall, and had since made them every kind of advances, but he soon perceived that he could not satisfy them except by ruining himself. The Duke César de Vendôme, son of Henri IV. and the Duchess de Beaufort, had early made the most lofty pretensions, and had shown himself as turbulent and factious as a legitimate prince. His life had been passed in rebellions and conspiracies, and in 1641 he had been forced to fly to England on the charge of an attempt to assassinate Richelieu. He did not return to France until after the death of the cardinal, and, as may well be imagined, he breathed nothing but vengeance against his memory. "He had much spirit," says Madame de Motteville, "and that was all the good that could be said of him."[1] To the ambition of the Vendômes, Mazarin skilfully opposed that of the Condés, who did not wish the aggrandizement of a house too near their own. They also owed it to themselves to sustain the Brézés, who had become their relatives by the marriage of Claire Clemence Maillé de Brézé, daughter of the duke and sister of

[1] Vol. i., p. 126.

the young and valiant admiral, with the Duke d'Enghien; so that Mazarin had little trouble in retaining the command of the fleet and of the principal maritime towns of France in faithful hands. But it was very difficult to preserve Brittany to the Meilleraies against the claims of a son of Henri IV., who had formerly possessed it, and who claimed it as a sort of family property. Mazarin therefore resigned himself to the sacrifice of La Meilleraie, but first he made it of the least possible value. He persuaded the queen to assume to herself the government of Brittany, and to appoint a lieutenant-general, evidently commissioned over the Vendômes, who should reside with La Meilleraie. The latter could not be offended at being second to the queen; and to arrange every thing so as to fully satisfy a personage of such consequence, Mazarin asked for him the title of duke which the late king had promised him, together with the reversion of the grand mastership of the artillery for his son—the same son to whom he afterwards gave with his name, his own niece, the beautiful Hortense.

Mazarin was much less inclined to favor the Duke de Vendôme, as he then had a dangerous rival with the queen in his younger son, the Duke de Beaufort, who was youthful, brave, possessing every appearance of loyalty and chivalry, and affecting a passionate devotion for Anne of Austria which was not at all displeasing to her. A few days before the death of the king, she had placed her children in his care. This mark of confidence inflated his vanity; he conceived hopes which he disclosed too plainly and which finally offended the queen, while at the same time to heighten his inconsistency, he assumed the chains of the beautiful but notorious Duchess de Montbazon. Besides, Beaufort did not even possess the semblance of a statesman; he had little talent, no secrecy, was incapable of application or of business, and only fit for some daring and violent deed. La Rochefoucauld portrays him thus:[1] "The one who had conceived the greatest hopes was the Duke de Beaufort; he had long been warmly attached to the queen. She had just given him a public token of her esteem by confiding the Dauphin and the Duke d'Anjou to his care on the day that the king received the extreme unction. The Duke de Beaufort, on his part, availed himself of this distinction and of his other advantages to bring himself into favor by affecting to believe that she was already firmly established in the government. He was large, well-made, enduring, and skilled in all kinds of exercises; he was haughty and audacious, but artificial in every thing and very unreliable; his wit was heavy and unpolished, though he often attained his ends through the artifice of his blunt manners; he was envious and malicious, and his valor, though great, was unequal." Retz does not, like La Rochefoucauld, accuse Beaufort of artifice, but he represents him as a presumptuous egotist of marked incapacity:[2] "M. de Beaufort had not even comprehended the idea of great designs, he had only aspired to them; he had heard them discussed among the Importants and had retained some of their jargon, and this, mixed with the expressions which he had borrowed verbatim from Madame de Vendôme,[3] formed a language which would have disfigured even the good sense of a Cato. His own was dull and scanty, and was also rendered more obscure by his conceit. He fancied himself able, and this it was that made him seem artful, for it is well known that he had not mind enough for intrigue. He possessed much personal courage, more, in fact, than often belongs to a blusterer." This portrait, exaggerated as it is after the manner of Retz, is nevertheless tolerably faithful; but at the beginning of the regency in 1643, the faults of the Duke de

---

[1] Ibid., p. 372.

[2] Vol. i., p. 216.

[3] Madame de Vendôme was a person of exalted piety, and who always spoke in the language of devotion.

Beaufort were not thus openly known, and they seemed to be eclipsed by his virtues. The queen only lost her liking for him by degrees. In the beginning of her friendship for him, she had offered him the place of grand-equerry, which had been vacant since the death of Cinq-Mars, and which would bring him in daily contact with her.[1] Beaufort had the folly to refuse this position, hoping for a better one; then, too late repenting his refusal, he asked it again, but in vain. The more his favor diminished, the more his irritation increased; and it was not long before he placed himself at the head of the enemies of the cardinal.

Madame de Chevreuse hoped to be more successful in asking the government of Havre for quite a different personage, of tried fidelity and the finest and rarest talents, La Rochefoucauld. She would thus have recompensed him for his services to the queen and to herself, have strengthened and enriched one of the chiefs of the party of the Importants, and have weakened Mazarin by taking an important command from a person of whom he was sure, the Duchess d'Aiguillon, niece of Richelieu. The cardinal succeeded in saving her without seeming to interfere in the matter. "This lady," says Madame de Motteville, "who, through her fine qualities, in many things surpassed ordinary women, knew so well how to defend her cause that she persuaded the queen that it was necessary for her own interests that she should leave her in command of this important place, saying that, having now none but enemies in France, her only safety and refuge was in the protection of her Majesty, who would always be the mistress of it; that, on the contrary, he to whom they wished her to give this government had too much talent, that he was capable of ambitious designs, and on the least discontent might join himself to some factious party, and that it was important for

---

[1] Mazarin himself gives us this fact, which has been hitherto ignored. ii. Carnet, pp. 72, 73.

the good of the State that she should keep this place under her own control for the king. The tears of a woman who had once been so proud moved the queen, who, after having reflected on her reasons, deemed it proper to leave things as they were."[1] It was Mazarin doubtless who suggested to the Duchess d'Aiguillon the sound and politic reasons which persuaded the queen, so well do they accord with the language which he continually holds towards her in his Carnets. Madame de Motteville says that he "confirmed her in her inclination to preserve Havre to the Duchess d'Aiguillon." Here, as in many other things, the art of Mazarin consisted in seeming simply to confirm the queen in the resolutions which he himself had suggested.

Observe that it is not we who attribute these various designs, this judicious and logical course of policy, to Madame de Chevreuse, but La Rochefoucauld, who ought to be correctly informed on the matter—indeed, he attributes it to her both in her own affairs and in that of the Vendômes.[2] Mazarin was not deceived by her; and more than once we read in his private notes these words: "My greatest enemies are the Vendômes, and Madame de Chevreuse who animates them." He also informs us that she had formed the design of marrying her daughter, the beautiful Charlotte, then sixteen years of age,[3] to the Duke de Mercoeur, the eldest son of the Duke de Vendôme, while his brother Beaufort was to have espoused the noble and amiable Mademoiselle d'Epernon, who, baffling these and many more brilliant schemes, buried herself at twenty-four in a convent of the Carmelites.[4] These marriages, which would have allied, strengthened, and united so many noble houses already but

---

[1] Vol. i., p. 136.

[2] Ibid., pp. 380–384.

[3] Charlotte Marie de Lorraine was born in 1627.

[4] *La Jeunesse de Madame de Longueville*, chap. i., pp. 99–105.

indifferently attached to the queen and to her minister, alarmed the successor of Richelieu, and he persuaded the queen to break them off secretly, finding trouble enough already from the marriage of the beautiful Mademoiselle de Vendôme with the brilliant and restless Duke de Nemours.[1]

When we follow attentively the details of the opposing intrigues of Madame de Chevreuse and of Mazarin, we know not to which to award the prize for skill, for sagacity, and for address. Mazarin knew how to make sacrifices enough to avoid making too many of them, treating everybody with circumspection, suffering no one to despair, promising a great deal, performing as little as possible, and lavishing homage and attentions upon Madame de Chevreuse herself, without ever deceiving himself as to her real sentiments. She, on her part, paid him back in the same coin. La Rochefoucauld says, that at this early period Madame de Chevreuse and Mazarin coquetted with each other. Madame de Chevreuse, who had always mingled coquetry with politics, seems to have essayed the power of her charms on the cardinal. The latter did not fail to lavish gallant words on her, and "even sometimes endeavored to make her believe that she inspired him with love." These are the precise words of La Rochefoucauld. There were some other women, too, who would not have been sorry to have won a little admiration from the prime minister. Among these was the Princess de Guymené, one of the most celebrated beauties of the French court, and not of a savage humor. She and her husband were friendly to Mazarin, despite all the efforts of Madame de Montbazon and Madame de Chevreuse, her mother and sister-in-law. It was evident, indeed, that Mazarin was very attentive to Madame de Guymené, and that he did not scruple to offer her, as well as Madame de Chevreuse, a thousand compliments; but he went no further, and the two beautiful women

[1] 1st Carnet, p. 112.

knew not what to think of so many flatteries and so much reserve. They sometimes jestingly asked each other which of the two he wanted; and as he made no advances, though all the while continuing his gallant protestations, "these ladies," says Mazarin, "conclude thence that I am impotent."[1]

This play lasted some time, but ended naturally on being carried into politics. Madame de Chevreuse grew impatient at obtaining nothing but words instead of any thing tangible and decisive. She had received a little money for herself, either in reimbursement of that which she had formerly loaned the queen, as we have seen in the preceding chapter,[2] or for the acquittal of the debts contracted during her exile and in the interest of Anne of Austria. At an early period, she had taken her friend and protégé, Alexandre de Campion, from the service of the Vendômes to place him in a suitable position in the household of the queen.[3] Châteauneuf had been reinstated in his office of chancellor of the royal orders, and his former government of Touraine was afterwards restored to him, after the death of the Marquis de Gèvres, who was slain in the month of August, before Thionville.[4] But

[1] III. *Carnet*, p. 39, "*Si esamina la mia vita e si conclude che io sia impotente.*"

[2] See Chapter II.

[3] *Recueil*, etc., letter of June 12, 1643: "I am now with the queen, who honors me by treating me with favor. I have all the *entrées*, and she has also bestowed a gift on me from which I have hopes of receiving nearly a hundred thousand crowns. Madame de Chevreuse, who is friendly with her, continues the confidence which she has always shown me."

[4] II. *Carnet*, p. 22: Journal of Olivier d'Ormesson, under the date of Aug. 30, 1643; and among the *Lettres françaises* of Mazarin, preserved at the *Bibliothèque Mazarine*, that of the 13th of August, in which the cardinal announces to Châteauneuf that the queen restores to him the government of Touraine. Another letter of January 2, 1644, terms him M. the Count de Châteauneuf, chancellor of the royal orders and governor of Touraine.

Madame de Chevreuse considered that this was doing but little for a man of the talent of Châteauneuf, who had staked his fortune and his life, and had suffered an imprisonment of ten years in the service of the queen. She perceived clearly that the perpetual postponement of the favors constantly promised to the Vendômes and to La Rochefoucauld, and as constantly deferred, were but so many artifices of the cardinal, and that she was his dupe; she complained loudly of this treatment, and began to indulge in bitter and sarcastic expressions against him. This was furnishing Mazarin with weapons against herself. He impressed the queen with the idea that Madame de Chevreuse wished to rule her, that she had but changed her mask and not her character, and that she was still the passionate and restless person who, with all her wit and her devotion, had never brought any thing but evil to the queen, and was only capable of ruining others and of destroying herself. By degrees, secret and hidden as it was, war was declared between them more openly. Rochefoucauld has admirably depicted the commencement and progress of this curious contest. The Carnets of Mazarin throw a new light on the subject, and infinitely exalt the talents of Madame de Chevreuse by showing to what degree Mazarin dreaded her.

Everywhere he regards her as the real chief of the party of the Importants. "It is Madame de Chevreuse," says he, unceasingly, "who animates them all."—"She studies to strengthen the Vendômes, she endeavors to gain all the house of Lorraine, she has already gained the Duke de Guise, and through him, she is attempting to win from me the Duke d'Elbeuf."—"She has a clear perception of every thing; she readily divines that it is I who am acting in secret on the queen to hinder her from restoring the government of Brittany to the Duke de Vendôme. She has said so to her father, the Duke de Montbazon, and also to Montagu."—"She quarrels with Montagu himself because he opposes Châteauneuf by sustaining Séguier, the present keeper of the seals."—"Madame de Chevreuse is not discouraged. She says that the affairs of Châteauneuf are not yet desperate, and that she asks but three months to show what she can do. She entreats the Vendômes to have patience, and sustains them by promising them a speedy change of scene."—"Madame de Chevreuse still hopes to cause my dismissal. The reason which she assigns for this is that when the queen refused to place Châteauneuf at the head of the government, she told her that she could not do it at present on my account, whence Madame de Chevreuse has concluded that the queen has much esteem and affection for Châteauneuf, and that when I am no longer there, the place is assured to her friend. From this arise the hopes and illusions which they cherish."—"The art of Madame de Chevreuse and the rest of the Importants consists in hindering the queen from hearing any conversation but that which is favorable to their party and directed against me, and in rendering every one suspicious to her who does not belong to them and who expresses any regard for me."—"Madame de Chevreuse and her friends openly assert that the queen will soon recall Châteauneuf, and by this they deceive everybody and induce those who are thinking of their future to go to him and to seek his friendship. They excuse the queen for the delay which she makes in giving him my place by saying that she still has need of me for some time longer."—"It is told me that Madame de Chevreuse secretly guides Madame de Vendôme, (a devotee who had much influence with the bishops and the convents,) and gives her instructions so that she may act rightly, and that all the machines employed against me may work well towards accomplishing their end."[1]

This last passage proves that Madame de Chevreuse, without being religious herself in the slightest degree, knew well how to avail herself of the party of devotees, which powerfully

[1] II. *Carnet*, pp. 65, 68, 75; III. Ibid., pp. 11, 19, 25, 29, 44.

influenced the mind of Anne of Austria and gave Mazarin much anxiety.

The chief difficulty of the prime minister lay in making Queen Anne—the sister of the king of Spain and herself possessing true Spanish piety—comprehend that it was absolutely necessary that, despite the engagements she had so often contracted, despite the urgent entreaties of the Court of Rome, and despite the solicitations of the chiefs of the episcopate, she should continue the alliance with Holland and the German Protestants, and persist in insisting on a general peace to be shared by our allies as well as ourselves, while the devotees were constantly repeating to her that she could make a partial peace and treat separately with Spain on most favorable terms, and that the scandal of an impious war between His Most Christian Majesty and the Catholic king would thus cease, and a much-needed relief be obtained for France. This was the policy of the former party of the queen. It was specious at least, and reckoned numerous partisans among the most enlightened and patriotic men. Mazarin, the disciple and heir of Richelieu, entertained higher thoughts which he was not yet willing to confide to Anne of Austria. He realized them by degrees, thanks to efforts unceasingly renewed and managed with infinite art; thanks most of all, to the victories of the Duke d'Enghien—for in every thing there is no more eloquent and persuasive advocate than success. However, the queen remained long undecided, and we see in the Carnets of Mazarin about the end of May, and through the months of June and July, that the great aim of the cardinal was to induce the regent not to abandon her allies, but to continue the war. Madame de Chevreuse, with Châteauneuf, defended the former policy of the party, and labored to win Anne of Austria back to it. "Madame de Chevreuse," says Mazarin, "causes it to be reported to the queen from every side that I do not wish for peace, that I have the same maxims as the Cardinal de Richelieu, and that to make a separate peace is both necessary and easy." He remonstrated often and earnestly against the dangers of such an arrangement, which would render useless the sacrifices of France during so many years. "Madame de Chevreuse wishes to ruin France!" he exclaims. He knew that, intimately allied with Monsieur, her former accomplice in every conspiracy plotted against Richelieu, she had persuaded him to the idea of a separate peace by holding out hopes to him of the marriage of his daughter, Mademoiselle de Montpensier, with the archduke, which would have obtained him the government of the Netherlands. He knew that she still retained all her influence over the Duke of Lorraine; and the Marshal de L'Hôpital, who commanded on that frontier, sent him word to distrust all the protestations of the Duke Charles, as he belonged wholly to Madame de Chevreuse. He knew lastly that she boasted of being able to effect a speedy peace through the Queen of Spain, whom she had at her disposal. He therefore entreated Queen Anne to repulse every proposal of Madame de Chevreuse, and to tell her plainly that she would not listen to any private arrangement, that she was determined not to separate herself from her allies, that she should insist on a general peace, that it was for this that she had sent ministers to Munster who were negotiating this important affair, and that it was useless to say any thing further on the subject.[1]

Repulsed at all these different points, Madame de Chevreuse would not yet own herself beaten. Seeing that she had employed insinuation, flattery, artifice, and every ordinary court intrigue in vain, her daring spirit did not recoil from the idea of resorting to other means of success. She continued to use the devotees and the bishops, and carried on her political plots with the chiefs of the Importants, while at the same time she attracted together that little cabal which formed in some sort the vanguard of the party, composed of

[1] III. *Carnet*, pp. 27, 43, 55.

men nurtured in the old intrigues, and accustomed to and always ready for surprises, who in former times had been engaged in more than one desperate enterprise against Richelieu, and who, in an extreme case, could be incited against Mazarin also. The memoirs of the time, particularly those of Retz and of La Rochefoucauld, describe them well. There were the Count de Montrésor, the Count de Fontrailles, the Count de Brion, the Count de Fiesque, the Count d'Aubijoux, the Count de Beaupuis, the Count de Saint-Ybar, Barrière, Varicarville, and many others beside,—impracticable spirits, intrepid hearts, of an unbounded fidelity to their cause and to their friends, professing the most ultra maxims, with a sort of worship for the unfortunate De Thou, continually invoking ancient Rome and Brutus, mingling amorous intrigues with all these, and urging themselves on in all their chimeras by the desire of pleasing the ladies. They gained the name of the *Importants* by their consequential airs, their affectation of ability and profundity, and their mysterious language.[1] Their chief favorite was the Duke de Beaufort, whom we already know, a personage of nearly the same stamp with themselves, made up at once of extravagance and of artifice, but professing great loyalty and devotion, and giving himself out as a man of action, and who, moreover, was wholly ruled by Madame de Montbazon, the youthful mother-in-law of Madame de Chevreuse. The former mistress of Chalais had no difficulty in gaining this little faction. She flattered it adroitly, while, with the art of a practised conspirator, she fomented

[1] To the well-known portraits of the Importants left us by Retz and La Rochefoucauld, may be added the following lines of Alexandre de Campion:—*Recueil.* "I have some friends who have not all the prudence that might be desired; they affect a passion for honor, and give to virtue so strange a garb, that it seems to me disguised; so that, though they may possess all its essential qualities, they use them so badly that the applause which they gain thereby, leads, perhaps, only to their destruction."

its spirit of false honor, of transcendental devotion, and of extravagant courage. Mazarin, who, like Richelieu, had an admirable police, warned by it of the movements of Madame de Chevreuse, understood the danger to which he was exposed. He well knew that she had not joined herself without design to men like these. He was perfectly informed of every thing that was said and done in their cabals. "They talk only among themselves of generosity and devotion," says he, in the notes which he wrote for the queen and himself; "they repeat without ceasing that one must know how to sacrifice himself for his cause; and it is Madame de Chevreuse who sustains and strengthens them in maxims so dangerous to the State."—"Saint-Ybar (one of those who, with Montrésor and Varicarville, had proposed to Monsieur and to Count de Soissons to rid them of Richelieu) is extolled by Madame de Chevreuse as a hero."—"Visit of Campion, a devoted servant of the lady."—"Madame de Chevreuse wishes to purchase one of the isles of the Loire in order to establish Campion on it, and to go there from time to time to have a secret interview with the Spanish agent, Sarmiento."—"Madame de Chevreuse animates them all. She says that, if they do not resolve to rid themselves of me, affairs will never be any better, that the nobles will be quite as much enthralled as formerly, that my power with the queen will continually increase, and that it is necessary to hasten to bring matters to a crisis before the Duke d'Enghien returns from the army."[1]

One could not be better informed, and the plan of Madame

---

[1] II. *Carnet*, p. 70: ". . . . Si predica siempre que es menester perdie se."—Ibid., p. 83: "Saint-Ibar portato dalla dama come un eroe."—III. Ibid., pp. 5, 24, 25: "Que los majores enemigos que yo tenia eran los Vandomos et la dama que li anima todos, diciendo que se no si teneria luogo la resolucion de deshacerse de my, los negotios (no) irian bien, los grandes serian tan sujetos come antes, y yo siempre mas poderia con la reyna, y que era menester darse prima antes que Anghien concluviesse."

de Chevreuse and the chiefs of the Importants was clearly laid open to the eyes of Mazarin; either by their incessant and skilfully concerted intrigues about the queen to cause her to abandon a minister for whom she had not yet openly declared herself, or to treat this minister as Luynes had treated the Marshal d'Ancre, and as Montrésor, Barrière, and Saint-Ybar had wished to treat Richelieu. The first part of the plan being unsuccessful, they began to think seriously of the second, and Madame de Chevreuse, the true head of the party, judiciously proposed to act before the return of the Duke d'Enghien, as the duke would protect Mazarin if at Paris; it was necessary, therefore, to profit by his absence to strike the decisive blow. Success seemed certain and even easy. They were sure of the people, who, wasted by a long war, and groaning beneath the weight of taxes, would joyfully welcome the hope of peace. They could count on the open support of the parliament, burning to regain that importance in the state which Richelieu had wrested from them, and which Mazarin disputed with them. They had the entire secret, and even public, sympathies of the episcopate, which, with Rome, detested the Protestant and demanded the Spanish alliance. They could not doubt the eager concurrence of the aristocracy, which still regretted its ancient and turbulent independence, and whose most illustrious descendants, the Vendômes, the Guises, the Bouillons, the Rochefoucaulds, were avowedly opposed to the rule of a foreign favorite, without fortune, without family, and as yet without glory. Even the princes of the blood resigned themselves to rather than loved Mazarin; Monsieur did not pride himself on an extreme fidelity to his friends, and the politic Prince de Condé would think twice on the subject before embroiling himself with the victors. He flattered all the parties by turns, but was only attached to his own interests. His son would act with his father, and they could gain him by loading him with honors. The next day there would be no resistance, and the day itself, scarce any opposition. The Italian regiments of Mazarin were with the army; there were scarcely any troops in Paris, except the regiments of the guards, of which nearly all the commanders, Chandenier, Tréville, and La Châtre, were devoted to the party. The queen herself had not yet renounced her former friendship. Even her prudence was misinterpreted. As she wished to be politic towards all and to satisfy all, she gave good words to everybody, and these good words were taken as tacit encouragements. She had not hitherto shown any great strength of character; though they believed indeed that she had some liking for the cardinal, and did not doubt the increasing force of an attachment of some months' standing.

On his side, Mazarin did not deceive himself. He could not yet have been master of the heart of Anne of Austria, since at this time, that is, during the month of July, 1643, he shows extreme disquietude in his most confidential notes. The dissimulation with which every one accused the queen alarmed him, and we see him pass through all the alternations of hope and of fear. It is curious to seize and follow the varying emotions of his soul. In his official letters to the generals and ambassadors,[1] he affects a security which he does not feel; with his intimate friends, he lets escape something of his perplexities, and they appear in his Carnets without disguise. In these we read the troubles of his mind in his passionate entreaties that the queen should declare herself. He feigns the most entire disinterestedness towards her, and only asks to give place to Châteauneuf if she has for him any secret preference. The ambiguous conduct of Anne of Austria drives him to despair, and he conjures her either to permit him to retire, or openly to declare herself in his favor.

"Every one says that Her Majesty has formed engage-

---

[1] See the valuable collection of French and Italian letters of Mazarin before cited, 5 vols. in fol., proceeding from Colbert, which are now in the *Bibliothèque-Mazarine*, Letters of 1642–1645, 1719, C.

ments with Châteauneuf. If this be true, let her Majesty tell me so. If she prefers to intrust her affairs to him, I will retire whenever she wishes." [1]—"They say that her Majesty is the greatest dissembler living, that no one can confide in her, that, if she seems to set any value on me, it is from sheer necessity, and that all her real confidence is in them." [2]—"If her Majesty wishes to retain me and to be benefited by me, she must throw off the mask, and give manifest tokens of the value that she sets on me." [3]—"I seek only the pleasure and the satisfaction of her majesty, but truth forces me to say that I cannot serve her as I ought with this perpetual anxiety, though I labor night and day to fulfil my duties." [4]—"It is certain that the Importants continue to assemble in the garden of the Tuileries, that those who style themselves the most devoted servants of the queen cry out against her government, that they are more than ever opposed to me, and always conclude by saying that, if they cannot destroy me by intrigue, they will attempt other means." [5]—"I receive a thousand warnings to take care of myself." [6]—"They inveigh against the queen more than ever. They are furious against Beringhen and Montagu. They say that the first practises a vile trade, and that they will give the second a beating; and that it is absolutely necessary to destroy all who are my friends." [7]—"I am told that

---

[1] II. Carnet, pp. 21, 22

[2] Ibid., p. 42.

[3] Ibid., p. 65: "Sy S. M. quiere conservar me de manera que puede ser de provechio a su servitio, es menester quitarse la maschera, y azer obras que declarase la protection que quiere tener de mi persona."

[4] Ibid., p. 77: "Es imposibile servire con estos sobresaltos, mientras trovajo di dia y de noche per complir a mis obligationes."

[5] Ibid., p. 76: "Es sierto que continuan juntarse al jardin de Tullieri que ablan contra el gobierno de la reyna los que se dicen sus majores serbidores, y que son contra my mas que nunca, hasta concluir siempre que sy per cabalas no podrano destruirme, intentaran otros modos."

[6] Ibid. p. 93: "Ricevo mille avvisi di guardarmi."

[7] III. Ibid., p. 18: "Los Importantes ablan contra la reyna mas que

there are so many incensed against me that it is impossible for me to avoid some great misfortune."[1]

He declares that he would retire willingly, if, by so doing, he believed that he could cause the storm to cease. "Ah!" exclaims he, "if the sea could be appeased by my sacrifice, I would cast myself into it as Jonah cast himself into the mouth of the whale."[2] He philosophizes sadly on the extreme difficulty of governing men, and especially Frenchmen, by reason and by the love of the public good. He consoles himself with the thought that he has not served France badly. In the beginning of his ministry, on the twenty-third of May, he had said to the queen: "Let her Majesty trust me during three months, and then let her do as she chooses."[3] Three months had not yet passed by, and France, victorious at Rocroy, was on the point of wresting from Austria the town which guarded the passage of the Rhine. Beyond the Alps, she was the arbiter of the differences of the Italian princes; the Pope himself recognized her mediation, despite the opposition of Spain; and in England, the king and parliament alike addressed themselves to her, to obtain her support.[4] Yet the chief author of this prosperity was calumniated, outraged, and menaced; and he knew not whether some officer of the guards or some one of

---

nunca. Estan desperados contra Belingan y Montagu; dicen que el primero es un alcahuete (maquereau), y que all' otro daron mil palos; que es menester perder todos los que fueran de mi parte."

[1] Carnet, p. 24: "Que muchas personas eran de manera animadas contra my que era imposibile que no me succediesse algun gran mal."

[2] II. Ibid., p. 76: "Sy la mar puede sosegarse con echarmi como Jonas en la bocca de la balena."

[3] I. Ibid., p. 108.

[4] III. Ibid., p. 65: "La riputazione della Francia non è in cattivo stato, poiche, oltre li progressi che dà per tutto fanno le armi sue, è arbitra S. M. delle differenze dei principi d'Italia, e di quelle del re d'Inghiltera con il parlamento, non obstante che li Spagnuoli faccino il possibile e combattino per ogni verso questa qualità, sino a minacciare il papa se adherisce alli sentimenti et alli mediazione di Francia."

the enthusiasts whom Madame de Chevreuse held at her disposal, was not reserving for him the fate of the Marshal d'Ancre. At the end of the month of June, he speaks in a letter to his friend, the Cardinal Bichy, just as he soliloquizes in the Carnets. "Every one sees," says he, "that I spare no fatigue, and that the crown has no more zealous, faithful, and disinterested subject than myself; yet I still think of returning to my own country when I can do so without being untrue to myself, to my duties, or to France; for although all my designs are good, although I protest that there is not one which has not for its object the glory of her Majesty, yet I unceasingly encounter a thousand obstacles and foresee greater ones yet in the future, the French having no real attachment to the good of the state, and holding all those in abhorrence who place it above their private nterests. Thus, I confess it to your eminence, I pass a most unhappy life, and were it not for the goodness of the queen, who gives me a thousand proofs of affection, I would endure it no longer." [1]

Nothing was changed at the end of July and in the beginning of the month of August, 1643, or rather, every thing was aggravated; the violence of the Importants increased daily; and though the queen defended her minister, yet she also treated with his enemies, and hesitated to take the decided attitude which Mazarin demanded of her, not only for his private interest, but also for that of the government. All at once an incident, seemingly insignificant at first, but gradually growing in importance, hastened the inevitable crisis, and forced the queen openly to declare herself, and Madame de Chevreuse to plunge still deeper into the fatal enterprise which had already entered her mind—we speak of the quarrel of Madame de Montbazon and Madame de Longueville.[2]

---

[1] *Bibliothèque Mazarine.* Italian letters of Mazarin, fol. 181: "30 giugno 1643."

[2] See *La Jeunesse de Madame d Longueville,* chap. iii., p. 225.

We have recounted this quarrel in detail elsewhere, and both ladies are known to the reader. Let us only observe that the Duchess de Montbazon, by her marriage with the father of Madame de Chevreuse, found herself the mother-in-law of Marie de Rohan, although younger than she, that the Duke de Beaufort was publicly a sort of attending cavalier to her, that the Duke de Guise paid her a very welcome court, and that she was thus allied on all sides to the Importants. Among her numerous lovers, she had counted the Duke de Longueville, whom she would gladly have retained, but who had just escaped her by espousing Mademoiselle de Bourbon. This marriage had greatly irritated the vain and selfish duchess; she detested Madame de Longueville, and blindly seized the first occasion which presented itself of carrying trouble into this new household. One evening, in her salon of the Rue de Béthizy or the Rue Barbette,[1] she picked up one or two letters in a woman's hand which some imprudent person had just let fall. With these she amused the whole company. The meaning of these letters was but too clear, and efforts were made to discover the author. The Duchess de Montbazon dared to attribute them to Madame de Longueville. This scandalous rumor spread rapidly, and the indignation of the hôtel de Condé may be imagined. Madame the Princess loudly demanded justice of the queen; and a reparation was exacted and agreed upon. The Duchess de Montbazon, forced to consent, apologized, but with a bad grace. A few days after, the queen having gone with Madame the Princess to the garden of Renard to a collation given her by Madame de Chevreuse, she found Madame de Montbazon there, and, when she entreated her to find some pretext for retiring in order to avoid a rencontre with Madame the Princess, the insolent duchess refused to obey. This offence, offered to the queen herself, could not remain unpunished, and the next day Madame de Montbazon

[1] For the hôtel de Montbazon, see Sauval, vol. ii., p. 124.

received an order to quit the court and repair to one of her estates near Rochefort. The friends and admirers of the lady uttered loud complaints; the whole party of Importants were roused, and the affair changed its aspect; from a private it became a general quarrel, as often in war a private engagement or a precipitate manœuvre involves a whole army and determines a battle.

It was difficult to be placed on worse ground. In the first place, the Duchess de Montbazon was as much despised for her manners and her character as celebrated for her beauty; and the object of her attack was a young woman who had but just appeared in society, and who was already the object of universal admiration; of a beauty so dazzling and ethereal that every one on seeing her compared her with an angel; of brilliant talents and a noble heart; the person, indeed, of all others, whom the Importants should have endeavored the most to gain, especially as her natural generosity did not lead her toward the side of the court, and had even given some umbrage to the prime minister. Madame de Longueville was then only occupied with wit, innocent coquetry, and, above all, the glory of her brother, the Duke d'Enghien. It must be confessed, however, that there were then in her heart some germs of an Important, which La Rochefoucauld afterwards knew but too well how to develop.[1] The injury which had been done her, the shameful

[1] About this time, or at least in the year 1644, Mazarin draws a severe portrait of Madame de Longueville, in which, if he does not calumniate her, he omits no blemish, pointing out all her defects without noticing her virtues, as though he already saw in her his most redoubtable enemy. V. *Carnet*, p. 23: "La detta Dama ha tutto il potere soprà il fratello. Fà vanità di disprezzare la corte, di odiare il favore, e disprezzar tutto quello che non vede a suoi piedi. Vorrebbe veder il fratello dominare e disporre di tutte grazie. È donna simulatissima; riceve tutte le deferenze e grazie come dovuteli. Vive d'ordinario con gran fredezza con tutti; ama la galanteria piu per acquistar servitori et amici al fratello che per alcun male; insinua nel fratello concetti alti alli quali per tanto egli è naturalmente portato; non fà conto della madre perche la crede

motives of which were apparent to every one, was revolting to all honorable hearts. The impetuosity of Beaufort on this occasion was also very blamable. He had formerly paid his addresses to Mademoiselle de Bourbon, who had repulsed them, so that his conduct bore an air of odious revenge. Besides, it was the policy of Madame de Chevreuse to deprive Mazarin of his supporters; it was for this that she had excited the devotees against him and made them act on the queen; now Madame de Longueville was not less the idol of the Carmelites and the devout party, than of the hôtel de Rambouillet. Lastly, the Duke d'Enghien, already covered with the laurels of Rocroy and on the point of adding to them those of Thionville, was so evidently the arbiter of the question, that Madame de Chevreuse earnestly insisted that they should rid themselves of Mazarin while the young duke was employed at a distance and before his return from the army. To wound him through a sister whom he adored, to incense him unnecessarily and hasten his return, was an extravagant folly; therefore all who were sensible among the Importants, La Rochefoucauld, La Châtre, and Alexandre de Campion, were anxious to pacify and hush up this unhappy quarrel; and Madame de Chevreuse, careful to make her court to the queen at the same time that she plotted a dark intrigue against her minister, had prepared a little festival at Renard, designed to dissipate the effects of what had just passed. But all her policy was foiled by the foolish pride of a woman as destitute of talent as she was of heart.[1]

---

troppo attaccata alla corte; crede con il fratello che tutte le grazie che si accordano alla sua persona, casa, parenti et amici li sieno dovute, e che si vorrebbe bene poter le negare, mà che non vi è corraggio di farlo per timore di disgustarli. Grande intelligenze con la marchesa di Sablè e duchessa di Lesdiguières. In casa di Sablè vi è un commercia continuo d'Andilly, la principessa di Ghimenè, Anghien, sua sorella, Nemur, e molti altri, e vi si parla di tutti liberamente. Bisogna haver qualcheduno là che possi avvertire di quello vi passerà."

[1] Alexandre de Campion, in the *Recueil* before cited, letter to Madame

Notwithstanding, Mazarin had profited by the blunders of his adversaries. At an early period he had joyfully seen, and had artfully increased, the enmity of the houses of Condé and Vendôme. In proportion as the Vendômes declared themselves more openly against him, he grew on better terms with the Condés. He had put to himself the question: "What must be done if the Vendômes and the Condés come to a rupture, presuming that the interest of the state be not involved in the quarrel?"[1]—a problem which he had evidently no difficulty in resolving, for the interest of the State and that of the cardinal were now united on the side of the Condés. At the same time that Madame de Montbazon and Beaufort offered this insult to Madame de Longueville, news came to Paris that the conqueror of Rocroy had just terminated the difficult siege of Thionville, and opened to France one of the gates of Germany. The sword of the young duke seemed everywhere to carry victory with it. The Marquis de Gèvres, who promised so fair, was slain; Gassion was grievously wounded; Turenne and Praslin were occupied in Italy; and Guébriant, closely pressed by Mercy, had just recrossed the Rhine. The Duke d'Enghien, with his boldness and his constantly increasing popularity, alone could exercise sufficient ascendency over the army to bring it back to Germany, and to dissipate the terror inspired by the memory of the defeat of Nortlingen. In the council, M. the Prince lent to Mazarin a selfish and wavering, yet essential and useful support. Madame the Princess was the best friend of the queen; she had openly declared herself in favor of the cardinal and against his rival Château-

---

de Montbazon: "If my advice had been followed at Renard, you would have departed in obedience to the queen; in which case you would not now be residing at Rochefort, and we should not be exposed to the danger that threatens us."

[1] III. *Carnet*, p. 100: "Come dovrei governarmi se nascesse querela trà il duca d'Enghien e la casa di Vendomo, senza che vi fosse intrigato il servitio della regina?"

neuf. To serve the Condés, therefore, was to serve the State, and also to serve himself. The choice of Mazarin could not be doubtful, and it is said that, far from soothing the queen, he incensed her the more.[1]

In this critical position, what course was left for Madame de Chevreuse to pursue? She endeavored to restrain Madame de Montbazon, but she could neither forsake her nor surrender herself. She therefore resolved to prosecute with energy the tragical scheme which had become the last hope, the final resource of the party. She had already broached the proposition of ridding themselves of Mazarin; and, through Madame de Montbazon, she had drawn Beaufort into it. The latter had gathered around him the men of action of whom we have spoken, and who were wholly devoted to him. A conspiracy had been formed, and all the measures concerted to surprise and kill the cardinal.

[1] Madame de Motteville, vol. i., p. 83.

CHAPTER IV.

AUGUST, 1643.

Conspiracy of Madame de Chevreuse and Beaufort against Mazarin.—La Rochefoucauld and Retz deny this Conspiracy.—Plan and Details of the whole Affair, as gathered from the Carnets and Letters of the Cardinal and the Memoirs of Henri de Campion.

WE need not be very much surprised at such an enterprise on the part of these two women and of a grandson of Henri IV. At this great epoch of our history, between the League and the Fronde, strength and energy were the distinctive traits of the French aristocracy. Court life and an effeminate opulence had not yet enervated them. Every thing there was extreme, vice as well as virtue. They attacked their enemies and defended themselves with the same weapons. The Marshal d'Ancre had been murdered, and the assassination of Richelieu had been more than once attempted, while he never hesitated to erect scaffolds in his turn. Was the trial of the Marshal de Marillac at Ruel under the cardinal's own eyes, his condemnation without conclusive proof, and his cruel execution on the Place de Grêve, any thing else than a judicial assassination? Corneille faithfully portrays the society of the times. His Emilie also enters into an assassination, yet she is represented as none the less perfect a heroine for it. Madame de Chevreuse had long been accustomed to conspiracies; she was fearless and unscrupulous, and she had not leagued herself with Beaupuis, Saint-Ybar, Varicarville, and Campion merely to pass her time in idle conversation. She had not remained a stranger to the designs which they had formerly plotted against Richelieu; in 1643, she fomented, as we have seen, their enthusiasm and devotion; and it is not without reason, we think, that Mazarin attributes to her the first idea of the project which was to have been accomplished by Beaufort.

As a matter of course, the Importants, and their successors, the Frondeurs, disavow this project, and give it out as an invention of the cardinal. This point is of the most vital importance, and merits a careful investigation. As it was this conspiracy, whether real or feigned, that decided the struggle between Madame de Chevreuse and Mazarin, history, under penalty of stopping at the surface of events and consenting to ignore their true causes, is bound to inquire whether Mazarin really owed the success of his whole career and the brilliant future which opened thenceforth before him to an ingenious and boldly maintained falsehood; or whether it was due to Madame de Chevreuse and the Importants, who, after having vainly essayed all other means against him, in an attempt to destroy him by the hand of the assassin, destroyed themselves and became unwittingly the instruments of his triumph. For ourselves, we are convinced, and we believe ourselves able to prove, that the conspiracy attributed to the Importants, far from being a chimera, was the almost inevitable *denouement* of the critical position which we have described.

La Rochefoucauld, without having shared in the insane hopes of his friends or lent his aid to their rash enterprise, makes it a point of honor to defend them[1] after their overthrow, and to cover their retreat. He affects to doubt whether the conspiracy that caused so much noise was real or imaginary. In his eyes, the Duke de Beaufort, by an injudicious stroke of policy, attempted to make the cardinal take the alarm, believing that it would only be necessary to terrify him to induce him to quit France; and that it was with this view

---

[1] *Memoires*, ibid., p. 388.

that he formed these assemblies and endeavored to give them an air of conspiracy. La Rochefoucauld especially constitutes himself the champion of Madame de Chevreuse, and professes himself fully persuaded that she was ignorant of the designs of the Duke de Beaufort. After the historian of the Importants, the memoirist of the Frondeurs holds nearly the same language. Like La Rochefoucauld, Retz has but one aim in his memoirs—that of giving himself a statesmanlike air, and of making a conspicuous figure in every thing, both good and evil. He is often more veracious, because he exercises less circumspection for others, and is more disposed to sacrifice everybody, himself excepted. We cannot comprehend his reserve or his incredulity in this instance. He knew very well that the most of those accused of having taken part in this plot had already been implicated in more than one similar affair. He has himself informed us that he had conspired with the Count de Soissons, that he had blamed him for not having struck Richelieu at Amiens, and that with La Rochepot, he, the Abbé de Retz, had formed the design of assassinating him at the Tuileries during the ceremony of the baptism of Mademoiselle. The coadjutorship of the archbishopric of Paris, which the regent had just granted him in consideration of the virtues and the services of his father, had pacified him, it is true, but his ancient accomplices, who had not been so well treated as he, had remained faithful to their cause, their designs, and their habits. Is Retz sincere when he refuses to believe that they attempted against Mazarin what he had seen them undertake and what he himself had undertaken against Richelieu? In his blind hatred, he throws all the blame on Mazarin, and pretends that he was or that he feigned to be afraid. According to him, it was the invention of Abbé de La Rivière, who, to deliver himself from the rivalry of the Count de Montrésor with the Duke d'Orleans, wished to persuade Mazarin that there was a conspiracy plotted against him in which Montrésor was concerned. It was also seconded by M. le Prince, who wished to destroy Beaufort in the fear that his son, the Duke d'Enghien, would engage in a duel with him, as he wished to do to avenge his sister, during the brief stay which he made in Paris after the capture of Thionville. Finally, Retz says: "The reason why I have never believed in this plot is that neither proof nor deposition indicative of it has ever been seen, although the greater part of the domestics of the household of the Vendômes have long been in prison. Vaumorin and Ganseville, to whom I have spoken of it a hundred times in the Fronde, have sworn to me that nothing could be more false: one of these was a captain of the guards, and the other, the equerry of M. de Beaufort.[1]

We shall presently see these last reasons—the only ones which merit any attention—dissipate of themselves; but let us commence by opposing to the two suspicious opinions of Retz and La Rochefoucauld some most disinterested witnesses, above all, the silence of Montrésor,[2] who, while protesting that neither he nor his friend, the Count de Bethune, had been implicated in the conspiracy imputed to the Duke de Beaufort, says not a single word against the reality of this conspiracy, which he would not have failed to ridicule had he believed it imaginary. Madame de Motteville, who is not in the habit of denouncing the unfortunate, after having related the different rumors of the court with impartiality, recounts some facts which seem authentic and decisive.[3] One of the best informed and most veracious of the contemporary historians does not express here the least doubt: "The Importants," says Monglat, "seeing that they could not expel the cardinal, resolved to rid themselves of him by the sword, and held several councils for this purpose at the hôtel de Vendôme."[4] This

---

[1] *Memoires*, vol. i., p. 65. See also the edition of M. Aimé Champollion, p. 41.

[2] *Memoires*, coll. Petitot, vol. lix.

[3] *Memoires*, vol. i., p. 184.

[4] *Memoires*, coll. Petitot, vol. lxix., p. 419.

opinion is confirmed by the new and numerous accounts furnished us by the Carnets of Mazarin and his confidential letters.

Let us disprove the supposition of Retz, that Mazarin may have been somewhat afraid, or that he feigned to be terrified by the shadow of a conspiracy. As to the courage of Mazarin, we appeal to La Rochefoucauld himself: "Unlike the Cardinal de Richelieu, who had a fearless mind and a timid heart, the Cardinal Mazarin," says he, "has more fearlessness of heart than of mind."[1] Mazarin had commenced as a soldier; he had given more than one proof of intrepidity, particularly at Casal, where he threw himself between two armies on the point of coming to blows. He doubtless studied to conjure down perils, but when he could not prevent them, he knew how to face them with firmness. Mazarin was not, therefore, a man to take alarm at false appearances; and, on the other hand, he had no need to feign imaginary fears, for the danger was certain; and, once more, in the constantly increasing progress of his credit with the queen, what resource remained to the Importants, except the enterprise which they had formerly attempted against Richelieu, and which they could easily renew against his successor? Mazarin had not as yet any guards, and he knew Madame de Chevreuse well enough to take in earnest the proposition which she had made in the cabals of the hôtel de Vendôme. Weigh well this consideration: in his Carnets, Mazarin is not on a stage; he is not writing for the public; he reveals his real feelings; and he is seen there, not intimidated, but aroused to a sense of his danger. He feels himself surrounded by assassins, and he is convinced that they are directed by Madame de Chevreuse. He follows all their movements, he gathers all their conversation, he collects the slightest proofs of their conspiracy, and he counts and names the chiefs and the soldiers.

---

[1] *Memoires*, ibid., p. 374.

"Madame de Chevreuse has brought in the brothers Campion."

"A host of men are brought in daily."

"Some enterprise is certainly on foot. They talk of surprising me in the Faubourg Saint Germain. They pretend to sell their horses in public and buy them in again in private.

"Plessis Besançon (a distinguished officer, commissary of stores and counsellor of state, and attached to Mazarin) says that more than forty armed men have been seen about the hôtel de Vendôme."

"M. de Bellegarde assures me that if I had not been in the carriage of his royal highness on my return from Maisons, Beaufort would have had me assassinated. The domestics of the Count d'Orval have seen twelve or fifteen men, armed with pistols, placed on three or four consecutive evenings between the hôtel de Créqui and their own in such a manner as easily to surprise and surround me."

"They have proposed to the Duke de Guise and his sons to assassinate me, but they would not listen to the proposal."

"L'Argentin met Beaufort and Beaupuis (the Count de Beaupuis, only son of the Count de Maillé) as they were returning from the Louvre, which the first had quitted when the queen retired to her oratory. 'My masters, there must certainly be some quarrel brewing,' said L'Argentin to them, 'for I just now met fifteen or twenty gentlemen on horseback, well mounted and armed with pistols.' 'Well, what have I to do with it?' answered Beaufort, shrugging his shoulders.—I have been warned that they mean to surprise me as I am going in my carriage to the palace of the Duke d'Orleans in the Faubourg Saint Germain, (the Duke d'Orleans had resided at the Luxembourg since the death of his mother, Marie de Medicis.)—On Wednesday, the Duke de Vendôme exclaimed twice while talking with the Marshal d'Estrées, 'I wish that my son Beaufort were dead.[1]' "

[1] III. *Carnet*, pp. 28, 34, 70, 82, 84, 85, and 91. IV. *Carnet*, p. 5.

These quotation, which we might easily multiply, prove incontestably that the conspiracy was a real one in the eyes of Mazarin. It was for this that he used every effort to throw light upon this dark intrigue. After some time, he submitted the affair to the ordinary course of justice in the court of all others the most independent and at the same time the least disposed in his favor, the Parliament of Paris. It was investigated in conformity with every formality of law, and in the most careful manner. Indications abounded, whatever Retz may say, and it was not the fault of Mazarin if conclusive proofs were wanting. But, promptly warned by the trusty friends which they possessed in the court, as well as about the queen and Mazarin himself, the Importants had no difficulty in favoring the escape of those conspirators most compromised in the affair.

"I am not very well satisfied with the Chevalier du Guet," says Mazarin,[1] "Brillet, Fouqueret, Lié, and twenty-four others have fled. It is supposed that they have embarked for England in a vessel which has been awaiting them for three weeks."[2] Far from letting them escape at their ease, Mazarin long pursued them with an obstinate eagerness, even into Holland. The 16th of April, 1644, he writes to Beringhen, who was then on a mission to the Prince of Orange, "Advices have been given me that Brillet and Fouqueret, who are the two persons deepest in the confidence of M. de Beaufort, and to whom he has most freely opened his heart concerning the conspiracy against my person, have gone to serve with the troops in Holland, having changed their names, and let their beards grow, so that they may not be known. Brillet is called La Ferrière. I entreat you to use all possible diligence to prove whether this is true, and when you return, to give an order to some person to watch over their actions, because we intend to devise some means of taking them."[3]

---

[1] III. *Carnet*, p. 88. [2] IV. *Carnet*, p. 8.

[3] *Lettres de Mazarin ; lettres françaises*, vol. i., fol. 274, recto.

The Count de Beaupuis, son of the Count de Maillé, he whom Mazarin designates in his Carnets and letters as the intimate confidant of Beaufort, and, after him, the principal person accused, found means of concealing himself during the first search; he succeeded in escaping from France, and sought an asylum at Rome under the avowed protection of Spain. Mazarin left no efforts untried to induce the court of Rome to send Beaupuis back to France, so that he might be legally adjudged. Not only did he make the demand officially through M. de Grémonville, then accredited to the holy see, but he wrote privately to all his sure friends, to the Cardinal Grimaldi, to his brother-in-law, Vincent Martinozzi, to Paul Macarani, and to Zongo Ondedei,[1] urging them to do all in their power to obtain the extradition of Beaupuis; and suggesting to them the strongest reasons which he charges them to plead to the holy father; namely, that Beaupuis was the principal confidant of Beaufort, that he was the link between Beaufort and the rest of the accused; that, this link being suppressed, justice could no longer take its course; that a crime was in question which ought particularly to affect the sacred college and the holy fathers—an assassination attempted on the person of a cardinal; that it was the queen herself who reclaimed Beaupuis; that it was a demand for one of her servants, Beaupuis being ensign in a company of horse-guards, a confidential post which demanded especial fidelity; and that Beaupuis would not be delivered to his enemies as was pretended, but to the parliament, whose impartiality was well known.

[1] *Lettres italiennes de Mazarin*, vol. i., letter to Ondedei, of March 25, 1645, fol. 226, verso; ibid., letter of May 8, to Vincenzo Martinozzi, fol. 240, verso; ibid., letter of May 26, to Paolo Macarani, fol. 246; ibid., letter of June 2, to Cardinal Grimaldi, fol. 248; ibid., letter to Ondedei, of the same date; ibid., letter to the Cardinal Grimaldi, of July 15, and to Ondedei of September 5; to the Cardinal Grimaldi, June 2, 1645, fol. 248; to Ondedei, June 2, 1645; to the Cardinal Grimaldi, July 15, 1645; to Ondedei, September 5, 1645.

The Pope could not at first forbear, for form's sake at least, from placing Beaupuis in the Chateau Saint-Ange. But he was soon liberated, and a private lodging given him where he could receive almost every one he chose. Mazarin loudly complained of such an indulgence. "All is arranged," says he, "so that if necessary he may be able to escape, or if not for this, to furnish the Duke de Vendôme with every facility for causing him to be poisoned, so that with Beaupuis may be destroyed the principal proof of the treason of his son. If all this happened in Barbary, how indignant we should be! Yet this passes at Rome, in the capital of Christendom, under the eyes and by the order of a pope!" Mazarin had sent a devoted agent named Gueffier to Rome, to receive Beaupuis from the hands of the holy father, with orders to take every imaginable means for preventing the escape of his prisoner on the way from Rome to Civita Vecchia, to put him on board a French vessel, and to bring him to France. He even went so far as to menace the protectors of Beaupuis with the vengeance of the young king, "who, though but seven years of age, has nevertheless very long arms." Mazarin did not cease his pursuit until the close of the year 1645, when he was clearly convinced that the new pope, Innocent X., who had succeeded to Urban VIII., as well as Pamphile, the cardinal-nephew, and Pancirolle, the secretary of state, belonged wholly to the Spanish party, and that France could expect neither favor nor justice from the pontifical court.

In default of Beaupuis, Mazarin would have been very glad to lay hands on one of the brothers Campion, who were intimately connected with Beaufort and with Madame de Chevreuse, and who stood too high in the confidence of both not to possess all their secrets. But he complains, as we have seen, of being very badly seconded. And then he had to deal with skilful conspirators, practiced in the art of sheltering themselves and hiding their tracks; with the active and indefatigable Duchess de Chevreuse, and with the Duke de Vendôme, who, to save his son, studied to favor the escape of all those whose depositions might have served to convict him, or guarded them in some sort himself, by concealing and even imprisoning them at Anet.[1] Mazarin was only able to seize obscure men, who were ignorant of the details of the plot and incapable of throwing any light on it. Notwithstanding, among these there were two noblemen, who, without having known this enterprise thoroughly, had at least been present at several assemblies which had been held under the plausible pretext of taking up the cause of the Duchess de Montbazon. Mazarin names them; they were MM. d'Avancourt and de Brassy, noblemen of Picardy, of tried courage, and intimate friends of Lié, captain of the guards of Beaufort, and one of the conspirators. Ganseville and Vaumorin, upon whose testimony Retz insists in order to prove that there never was any conspiracy, were of no importance. Vaumorin may have become captain of the guards of the Duke de Beaufort in 1649, but he was not so in 1643, it was Lié; and Ganseville was one of those subordinates who had never been admitted to his confidence. They knew nothing; they may, therefore, have very truly said to Retz during the Fronde, what he makes them say. But D'Avancourt and De Brassy did know something, and it was for this reason that the Duke de Vendôme entreated them to come to Anet. Arrested and thrown into the Bastille, and intimidated or gained over, whatever Retz may say of it, they made grave depositions and furnished conclusive evidence; but these stopped at Henri de Campion and Lié, the only conspirators whom they had known. Mazarin neglected nothing to draw out and make use of the only important capture which he had made. "Hasten the examination of the two prisoners," says he. "Summon the proprietor of the Maison du Sauvage, situated next the hôtel de Vendôme, where D'Avancourt and De Brassy lodged, as well as the innkeeper

---

[1] IV. *Carnet*, p. 8.

near the river, at whose house there were eleven persons on Monday evening. Question the lackeys of the aforesaid D'Avancourt and Brassy, etc." "The brother of Brassy says that the Duke de Vendôme is displeased with them because they suffered themselves to be taken without resistance."[1] The Importants were much disquieted for fear of some revelations which the two prisoners might make. Mazarin spread the report that Avancourt and Brassy had said nothing of importance, and that the affair would end in nothing, in order to lull the vigilance and the fears of the fugitives, and embolden them to leave their retreat, and come to be captured at Paris. "Tremblay "[2] (the governor of the Bastille) "has told me that Limoges (Lafayette, the Bishop de Limoges, one of the chiefs of the Importants in the Church) bears me much malice, and that he has begged to know what the two prisoners have said, ending by saying that the Cardinal Mazarin would be finely hoaxed, and that he had only caused them be arrested and thrown into the Bastille in order to seem to justify the injury done to the Duke de Beaufort. I have ordered Tremblay to tell Limoges that the two prisoners made no confession, but defended themselves very plausibly, in order to confirm him in the opinion which he holds, so that, on giving this information

[1] At Paris, no one doubted but the affair of these two gentlemen was seriously prosecuted. A very curious private correspondence, preserved in the archives of foreign affairs, FRANCE, vol. cv., contains a letter from a person called Gaudin to Servien, the skilful diplomatist, under date of October 31, 1643, in which the following passage is found, which repeats almost verbatim the words of the Carnets: "Search has been made in the inns of the Faubourg Saint Germain, where the two gentlemen now imprisoned in the Bastille lodged. On seeing that nothing could be discovered from their examination nor that of their lackeys, the hosts and hostesses of the said inns, namely, of the Sauvage and of some other, were also imprisoned, in the hope to intimidate them and draw from them some confession of the deed of which they are accused; this availed nothing, and they have been released."

[2] IV. *Carnet*, p. 9.

to the Duke de Vendôme, as he will not fail to do, those who have fled will be reassured and return, and thus enable me to lay hands on some one of them."

But why exhaust ourselves in demonstrating that Mazarin enacted no farce in the suit instituted against the conspirators, that he pursued them in good faith and with vigor, and that he was fully convinced that a project of assassination had been formed against him, when the truth of the existence of such a project is elsewhere evinced, and when, in default of a sentence of parliament which must, necessarily, have come to a stand from want of sufficient proofs, neither Beaupuis, nor any of the Campions, nor Lié, nor Brillet having been taken, we have what is still better, namely, the full and entire avowal of one of the principal conspirators, with the plan and details of the whole affair, disclosed in memoirs too recently known, but whose authenticity cannot be contested.[1] We speak of the valuable memoirs of Henri de Campion, brother of the friend of Madame de Chevreuse, whom the latter had induced to enter with him into the service of the Duke de Vendôme, and more particularly, of the Duke de Beaufort. Henri had accompanied the duke in his flight to England after the conspiracy of Cinq-Mars, and had returned with him; he possessed his entire confidence, and he recounts nothing in which he himself has not taken a considerable part. Henri was of a very different character from his brother Alexandre. He was well-informed, honorable, and courageous, no braggart, averse to all intrigues, and born to make his way in the career of arms by the most direct paths. He wrote his memoirs in the solitude in which, after the loss of his wife and daughter, he awaited death in the midst of exercises of the most fervent piety. It is not in this mood that one is apt to invent fables, and there is no

---

[1] Memoires de Henri de Campion, etc., 1807, à Paris, chez Treuttel et Wertz, in 8vo. Petitot has only given an extract from them in the sequel of the Memoires de la Châtre, vol. li. of his collection.

medium—his assertions are such that they must be implicitly believed, or, if their truth is doubted, he must be considered as the basest of villains. No interest could have guided his pen; for he composed, or at all events completed his memoirs shortly after the death of Mazarin, without thinking therefore of making court to him by tardy revelations, and scarcely two years before his own death, which took place in 1663. Truly, he may be said to have written in the fear of God and under the sole inspiration of his own conscience.

Now open his memoirs and you will see there all the details which fill the Carnets of Mazarin confirmed point by point. Nothing is wanting; every thing is in accordance with them; they correspond marvellously. It seems in truth as if Mazarin, in writing his notes, must have had before his eyes the memoirs of Henri de Campion, or as if Henri de Campion had copied verbatim from the Carnets of Mazarin—so well does he both complete and recapitulate them.

His brother Alexandre, in his letters, written during the month of August,[1] lets fall more than one mysterious sentence. He writes thus to the Duchess de Montbazon, "You must not despair, madame; there are half a dozen honest men who have not yet yielded. Your illustrious friend will not forsake you. If it be necessary to renounce your friendship to be considered sane, there are some who will choose rather to pass for madmen all their lives." Like Montrésor, he does not once say that no plot had been formed against Mazarin, which is a sort of tacit avowal of it; and when the storm bursts, he resolves to conceal himself, counsels Beaupuis to do the same, and concludes with these significant words, "We cannot engage in the affairs of the court and be masters of their results, and as we profit by the good, we must also resolve to endure the evil." Henri de Campion lifts this already transparent veil.

---

[1] *Recueil* before cited.

He explicitly declares that there was a project for ridding themselves of Mazarin, and that this project was originated, not by Beaufort, but by Madame de Chevreuse, in concert with Madame de Montbazon. "I believe," says he, "that the duke's design was not prompted by his own private feelings, but by the persuasions of the Duchesses de Chevreuse and De Montbazon, who had entire power over him, and who bore an irreconcilable hatred towards the cardinal. The reason why I say this is that all the while that he was pursuing it, I detected in him a secret repugnance to it, which, if I mistake not, was overruled by the promise that he had probably made these ladies." There had therefore really been a plot, and its true author, as Mazarin asserts and as Campion repeats, was none other than Madame de Chevreuse, for Madame de Montbazon was but a tool for her.

Beaufort, being gained over, persuaded his intimate friend, Count de Beaupuis, son of the Count de Maillé, and ensign in the horse-guards of the queen. Madame de Chevreuse added to them Alexandre de Campion, the eldest brother of Henri, with whom we are already acquainted. "She had much love for him," says Henri de Campion, in a manner which, added to the ambiguous words of Alexandre which we have quoted before,[1] strengthens the suspicion whether he was not at that time really one of the numerous successors of Chalais. He was then thirty-three years of age, and his brother admits that he had contracted the tastes and habits of the faction from the Count de Soissons. Beaupuis and Alexandre de Campion approved the plot which was communicated to them, "the first," says Henri de Campion, "believing it to be a means of attaining higher offices, and my brother seeing therein the advantage of Madame de Chevreuse, and consequently, his own."

Such were the two first accomplices of Beaufort. Soon

---

[1] See Chapter II.

after, he disclosed his plans to Henri de Campion, one of his principal gentlemen, to Lié, captain of his guards, and to Brillet, his equerry. There the secret rested. Many other gentlemen and servants of the house of Vendôme were to have participated in the action, but they were not made confidants; whence we understand the ignorance of Vaumorin and Ganseville, and the assertion which they may have made to Retz during the Fronde. The affair was well planned and worthy of Madame de Chevreuse. There were but five or six conspirators admitted to full confidence, all well capable of keeping the secret, and they kept it faithfully. Under them were the men of deeds, who were ready for action but knew not what they were to do; and beyond these were the men of the morrow, upon whom they counted to applaud the blow, when it had been struck, without deeming it proper to take them into the conspiracy. At all events, Henri de Campion does not even name Montrésor, Béthune, Fontraille, Varicarville, and Saint-Ybar, which explains why Mazarin, although having had an eye on them all, did not cause their arrest. Neither does Henri de Campion speak of Chandenier, La Châtre, Tréville, the Duke de Guise, the Duke de Retz, the Duke de Bouillon, and La Rochefoucauld, whose sentiments were not doubtful, but who were not ripe for imbruing their hands in an assassination; this also explains the silence of Mazarin in respect to them in all that concerned the conspiracy of Beaufort, although he did not deceive himself in the slightest degree as to their disposition and the part which they would have taken if the conspiracy had succeeded, or even if a serious struggle had been commenced.

The plot rested for some time with Madame de Chevreuse, Madame de Montbazon, Beaufort, Beaupuis, and Alexandre de Campion. The final resolution was not taken until the end of July or in the beginning of August; that is, precisely at the height of the quarrel between Madame de Montbazon and Madame de Longueville, which urged on the crisis and opened the door to all the following events. It was then that Beaufort spoke of it to Henri de Campion in the presence of Beaupuis. The crime of Mazarin was that of continuing the policy of Richelieu. "The Duke de Beaufort said to me that he presumed I had remarked that Cardinal Mazarin was re-establishing the tyranny of the Cardinal de Richelieu, both in the court and throughout the whole kingdom, with even more authority and violence than had been seen under the government of the latter; that, having entirely gained the mind of the queen and won all the ministers to his disposal, it was impossible to check his evil designs without taking his life; and that, regard for the public good having made him resolve to take this course, he therefore acquainted me with it, praying me to assist him by my counsels and my personal aid in its execution. Beaupuis then took up the discourse, warmly representing the evils which the too great authority of the Cardinal de Richelieu had brought upon France, and concluding by saying that similar ills must be prevented before his successor should have had time to render them incurable." In conclusion, these are the views and the words of the Importants and the Frondeurs, of La Rochefoucauld and of Retz. Henri de Campion asserts that at first he opposed the project of the duke with so much earnestness that he wavered more than once, but that the two duchesses soon incensed him again, while Beaupuis and Alexandre de Campion urged him on instead of restraining him. Some time after, Beaufort having declared that he was fully resolved in the matter, Henri de Campion yielded on two conditions. "One was," says he, "that I should not be required to lay hands on the cardinal, as I would kill myself rather than do an act of this sort; and the other, that if the execution should be attempted in Beaufort's absence, I should not be there, while if he himself were present, I should not scruple to remain near his person, to defend him in any accidents that might happen; my employ near him and my affection for him alike obliging me to this.

He granted me these two things, professing to esteem me the more for them, and adding that he should certainly be at the execution in order to authorize it by his presence."

The plan was to attack the cardinal in the street while he was making calls in his carriage, at which time he usually had with him but a few ecclesiastics, together with five or six lackeys. They were to appear suddenly with an armed force, surround the carriage and strike Mazarin. For this, it was necessary that a certain number of adherents of the house of Vendôme should be found every day in the cabarets around the residence of the cardinal, which was then in the hôtel de Clèves, near the Louvre. Henri de Campion names Ganseville positively as among the followers who had not been admitted into the secret. To these he adds " MM. d'Avancourt and de Brassy, the Picardians, both determined men and intimate friends of Lié." They gave as a pretext that the Condés intending to offer an affront to Madame de Montbazon, the Duke de Beaufort wished to have a troop of armed and mounted gentlemen at his command to defend her. The characters were distributed in advance. Some were to stop the coachman of the cardinal; others were to open the doors and strike the fatal blow; while the duke was to be there on horseback with Beaupuis, Henri de Campion and others, to oppose and disperse all who attempted to resist them. Alexandre de Campion was to remain near the Duchess de Chevreuse and subject to her orders, while she was to be more than usually assiduous about the queen, to pave the way for her friends, and in case of success, to win her over to the side of the victors. Several favorable occasions for executing this plan presented themselves. At one time, Henri de Campion being with his retinue in the little Rue du Champ-Fleury, one end of which issues into the Rue Saint-Honoré, and the other, near the Louvre, he saw the cardinal leave the hôtel de Clèves in a carriage with the Abbé de Bentivoglio, nephew of the celebrated cardinal of that name, together with some monks and a few valets. Campion asked one of them where the cardinal was going; he answered, to the hôtel of the Marquis d'Estrées. "I saw," says Campion, "that if I chose to give this intelligence, his death was certain. But I believed that in so doing I should be so culpable both before God and man that the occasion did not tempt me."

The next day it was known that the cardinal was to go to partake of a collation with Madame du Vigean, at her charming villa of La Barre, at the entrance of the valley of Montmorency, at which the queen, who had already departed, together with Madame de Longueville, would be present.[1] The cardinal proceeded thither, having no one in the carriage with him but the Count d'Harcourt. Beaufort commanded Campion to summon his troop and pursue him, but Campion represented to him that if they attacked the cardinal in the company of the Count d'Harcourt, they must decide to kill both, D'Harcourt being too generous to see Mazarin struck down before his eyes without defending him, and that the murder of D'Harcourt would excite all the house of Lorraine against them.

A few days after, they received information that the cardinal and the Duke d'Orleans were going to dine at Maisons with the Marshal d'Estrées. "I persuaded the duke to consent," says Campion, "that if the minister should be in the carriage of his royal highness, the design should not be executed; but he said that, if he were alone, he must die. In the morning, he caused horses to be prepared, and remained in the Capucins with Beaupuis, near the hôtel de Vendôme, posting a footman in the street to inform him when the cardinal should pass, and enjoining on me to stay with the conspirators assembled daily by my orders at the Angel, (the name of a cabaret,)

---

[1] See *La Jeunesse de Madame de Longueville*, chap. ii., p. 178, and chap. iii., p. 233. This, probably, is the same party of pleasure which Scarron describes, vol. vii., p. 178, *Voyage de la Reine à La Barre.*

in the Rue Saint-Honoré, near the hôtel de Vendôme, and, if the cardinal should go without the Duke d'Orleans, to mount together with all these gentlemen, and attack him when passing the Capucins. "I was in the utmost anxiety," adds Campion, "until, on seeing the carriage of the Duke d'Orleans pass, I perceived the cardinal in the back with him."

Finally, the irritation of Beaufort having been carried to its height by the banishment of Madame de Montbazon, which without question took place on the 22d of August;[1] and spurred on moreover by Madame de Chevreuse, by passion, and by a false sense of honor, the duke himself became impatient for action. Seeing that in the daytime he constantly encountered difficulties the cause of which he was very far from divining, he resolved to strike the blow during the night, and arranged an ambuscade which Campion has described to us. The cardinal went every evening to the palace of the queen, and returned quite late. They resolved to attack him on his return between the Louvre and the hôtel de Clèves. Horses were to be in readiness at some neighboring inn, and the duke himself was to stay there with Beaupuis and Campion while the minister was with the queen. As soon as he departed, the three were to advance and summon the others, who, meanwhile, were to remain mounted on the quay, by the side of the river, near the Louvre. All this could easily be done under cover of the night, without awakening any suspicion.

Reflect that he who furnishes these precise details was one of the principal conspirators, that he writes at a sufficient distance from the event, in safety, and, let us say once more, disinterestedly, fearing nothing more from Mazarin who has just died, and expecting nothing from him; reflect that in speaking as he does, he accuses his own brother; that, though he doubtless attributes to himself laudable intentions and even

[1] See in *La Jeunesse de Madame de Longueville*, chap. iii., p. 226, the lettre de cachet addressed to Madame de Montbazon.

some good deeds, he nevertheless confesses that he had entered into the plot, and that, if the execution had taken place, he would have shared in it, by fighting at the side of Beaufort. The suit instituted before parliament having been broken off for want of proofs, Campion did not suppose that Mazarin had ever known "the circumstances of the plot, nor who they were that knew it to the bottom and were concerned in it." He says also that, "now that the cardinal is dead, there is no longer any fear of injuring any one by telling things as they are." He does not, therefore, defend himself; he believes himself sheltered from all pursuit, and he only writes to relieve his conscience. Now what he says is precisely the same that Mazarin, on his side, had drawn from his various informants.

We have seen what importance Mazarin attached to the arrest of D'Avancourt and De Brassy, and what art he used in spreading the report that they had disclosed nothing in their examination, in order to remove all anxiety from those whom they might have compromised, and thus to draw them to Paris, where they would not fail to be taken. Henri de Campion assures us that he was especially in question, and really seems to be translating into French one of the Italian passages of the Carnets. "Avancourt and Brassy were taken to the Bastille," says he, "where they deposed that I had summoned them several times in behalf of the Duke de Beaufort for the interests of Madame de Montbazon as I had told them. This furnished no pretext for examining the duke, as they confessed that he had not spoken to them; he did not fail, therefore, to deny having given the orders which I had carried to them in his behalf; it was evident from this, that his trial could not be proceeded with until I had been taken, and matter found from my own depositions whereon to question him and to embarrass us both, and thus to discover some trace of the affair. The proofs of this conspiracy were of essential importance to the cardinal, who, wishing only to establish himself in the government, and affecting to do so by gentleness, was very sorry to be obliged, in the beginning, to do violence to one of the greatest men of the kingdom for his private interest, without showing a reason which compelled him to treat the duke with such rigor. In despair at being unable to convince the others of that of which he himself was fully certain, he wished much to have me in his hands. He judged, however, that it was necessary to give me time to reassure myself in order to seize me with greater facility."

We can add to all this that Henri de Campion, after being pursued and closely pressed in his retreat at Anet, the house of the Duke de Vendôme, having fled from France to Rome to find his friend, the Count de Beaupuis, recounts the persevering efforts which Mazarin made to obtain the extradition of the latter, the resistance of Pope Innocent X., and the regard which he had for Beaupuis when he was forced to place him in the Chateau Saint-Ange; facts which, being found both in the Carnets and letters of Mazarin and in the memoirs of Henri de Campion, place the sincerity of the movements of the cardinal and the exactness of his information beyond a doubt.

Is not this sufficient to reduce to nothing the interested doubts of La Rochefoucauld and the impassioned denials of the chief of the Fronde, the very spiritual but very unveracious Cardinal de Retz, the most bitter and the most obstinate of all the enemies of Mazarin? As to ourselves, it seems to us either that there is no longer any reliance to be placed upon history, or that we must henceforth regard it as a point fully demonstrated that there was a plot for the assassination of Mazarin which was foiled, that this plot was originated by Madame de Chevreuse and in some sort forced upon Beaufort by her and Madame de Montbazon, that Beaufort's principal accomplices were the Count de Beaupuis and Alexandre de Campion, that Henri de Campion afterwards entered into the affair at the urgent solicitation of the duke, as well as two other officers of a subordinate rank, that during the month of August there were several attempts at its execution, the final one of which was made after the exile of Madame de Montbazon on the last of August or rather the first of September, and that this last attempt only failed through circumstances wholly independent of the will of the conspirators.

CHAPTER V.

SEPTEMBER, 1643–1679.

Failure of the Conspiracy.—Arrest of Beaufort and exile of Madame de Chevreuse to Anjou.—New intrigues.—Madame de Chevreuse fears imprisonment, and quits France for the third time in 1647.—Her capture and subsequent release by the English Puritans.—She takes refuge at Liège.—Returns to Paris in 1649.—Her *rôle* in the Fronde.—Her reconciliation with the queen and with Mazarin.—She contributes to the downfall of Fouquet and the rise of Colbert.—Her death in 1679.

WHAT of the last plan of assassination formed against Mazarin—the nocturnal ambuscade, so well arranged for the 1st of September, 1643, did it also fail? In answer, without stopping to discuss the conjectures of Henri de Campion, we will confine ourselves to saying that Mazarin, who was on his guard, avoided the destined blow by staying away from the queen's palace on the evening when he was to have been stabbed on his return from the Louvre. The next morning, the scene was changed. The rumor was spread that the prime minister had narrowly escaped being slain by Beaufort and his friends on the night before, but that fortune had declared itself in his favor. A project of assassination, especially when it has failed, always excites extreme indignation, and he who has escaped a great danger and seems destined to come off victorious, has no difficulty in finding supporters. A host of men who would, perhaps, have seconded Beaufort had he been successful, came now to offer their services and their swords to the cardinal, and in the morning he repaired to the Louvre escorted by three hundred noblemen.

For some days past, Mazarin had felt that it was necessary at all risks to clear up his position and to force the queen to declare herself openly. The moment was a decisive one. If the danger which he had just shunned and which was even now suspended over his head was not sufficient to draw the queen from her indecision, it was because she had no love for him; and Mazarin well knew that in the midst of the dangers that surrounded him, his whole power lay in the affections of the queen, and that on her depended both his present and his future safety. Thus, either through policy or through sincere passion, he always addressed himself to the heart of Anne of Austria, and he soliloquized thus at the outset of the contest: "If I thought the queen only made use of me through necessity, without having any personal regard for me, I would not stay here three days."[1] But, as we have sufficiently proved, Anne of Austria loved Mazarin. Every day, on comparing him with his rivals, she appreciated him the more. She admired the precision and clearness of his intellect, his subtlety and his penetration, the capacity for labor which enabled him to bear the weight of the government with almost superhuman ease, his keen perception, his consummate prudence, and, at the same time, the judicious energy of his resolutions. She saw the affairs of France everywhere prospering in his firm and able hands. The cardinal had had no share, it is true, in the great battle which had just inaugurated the new reign with so much eclat; but he had had much to do with the success which followed it and which proved to astonished Europe that the day of Rocroy was not merely a happy accident. When every one in the council was opposed to the siege of Thionville, when M. the Prince himself was averse to it, when Turenne, being consulted, dared not declare himself in its favor, it was Mazarin who had insisted with more than usual vehemence

---

[1] III. *Carnet*, p. 10, in Spanish, "Sy yo creyera lo que dicen que S. M. se sierve di mi per necessidad, sin tener alguna inclination, no pararia aqui tres dias."

that they should profit by the victory of Rocroy, and bring France to the banks of the Rhine. The first proposition, without doubt, came from the young conqueror, but to Mazarin belongs the credit of comprehending it, sustaining it, and securing its ultimate triumph. If never had prime minister been served by such a general, never either had general been served by such a prime minister; and thanks to both, on the 11th of August, while messieurs, the Importants, were employing their talents in offering a base affront to the noble sister of the hero who had just saved France and was now on the point of extending its territories—while they were displaying their eloquence in the *salons* or whetting their daggers in dark cabals, Thionville, then one of the chief strongholds of the Empire, surrendered after an obstinate defence, thus enabling our armies to march to the assistance of Guébriant, cover Alsatia, cross the Rhine, and go to cope with Mercy. The regency of Anne of Austria was opening under the most brilliant auspices. Yet, notwithstanding all this, the minister to whom the queen owed so much, instead of obtruding himself on her and pretending to a right to rule her, was at her feet, lavishing attentions, respect. and affection on her such as she never before had known. Far from perceiving any resemblance to the imperious and moody Richelieu, she could recall with pleasure the words of Louis XIII. when he presented Mazarin to her for the first time in 1639 or 1640, "He will please you, Madame, because he resembles Buckingham." But he was a Buckingham of a very different stamp. She could not but have shuddered when Mazarin placed before her eyes all the proofs of the odious conspiracy that had been formed against him. There must have been full explanations between them. More than ever he must have urged her to throw off the mask,[1] to sacrifice the circumspection which she had studied to preserve to what was now become a manifest

[1] II. *Carnet*, p. 65: "Quitarse la maschera."

necessity, to brave the censures of a few devotees, and in short to give him permission to defend his life. Hitherto, Anne of Austria had hesitated for reasons which are self-evident. The insolence of Madame de Montbazon had already irritated her greatly; the conviction which she now acquired of the numerous attempts at assassination which had failed by chance, and which at any time might be renewed, at length decided her, and it is at the close of the month of August that we must fix the positive date of the declared, public, and unrivalled ascendency of Mazarin over Anne of Austria. He had never been displeasing to her; her partiality for him commenced in the month preceding the death of Louis XIII.; in the month of May she appointed him prime minister, partly from regard and more from policy; this regard increased by degrees until it grew strong enough to resist all attacks on it; these attacks, by proceeding to the utmost violence, and making her fear for his life, precipitated the victory of the happy cardinal, and on the day after the nocturnal ambuscade in which he was to perish, Mazarin became the absolute master of the heart of the queen, and more powerful than ever Richelieu had been after the day of Dupes.

We have sought in vain in the Carnets of Mazarin for some traces of the explanations which Mazarin must have had with the queen at this critical juncture. These explanations probably were not such as to be so easily forgotten as to require one to keep notes of them. However, we find an obscure passage written in Spanish, from which we glean the following words: "I ought no longer to have any doubts, since the queen, in an excess of goodness, has told me that nothing can deprive me of the post near her person which she has done me the favor to give me; notwithstanding, as fear is the inseparable companion of affection,"[1] etc. About this time, Mazarin being somewhat

[1] III. *Carnet*, p. 45: "—— mas contodo esto siendo el temor un compagnero inseparabile dell' affection," etc.

indisposed by reason of his labors and cares, and suffering from the jaundice, wrote this line which is very short, but which furnishes food enough for thought: "The jaundice, fruit of extreme love."[1]

Madame de Motteville was on duty near Queen Anne, when, at the report of the abortive attempt at assassination, the courtiers hastened to the Louvre to protest their devotion. The queen, greatly excited, said to her,[2] "You shall see before twice twenty-four hours have passed, how I will avenge myself for the tricks which these false friends have played on me." "Never," says Madame de Motteville, "will the memory of these few words be effaced from my mind; I saw at that moment from the fire which burned in the eyes of the queen, and from the things which happened in truth on the same evening and the next day, what a sovereign is when she is in anger, and how capable she is of doing all that she wills." If the faithful maid of honor had been less discreet, she might have added: especially when the sovereign is a woman, and in love.

Mazarin had said:[3] "The plots against me will never cease so long as my enemies see near her Majesty a powerful party declared against me, and capable of gaining the mind of the queen if any defeat should happen to me." The overthrow of this party was demanded by Mazarin and granted by Anne of Austria, and the most energetic measures were immediately resolved on.

That which was of all others the most pressing, and which could not be deferred for a single day, was to screen himself from all new assassins, and to profit by the first burst of popu-

---

[1] IV. *Carnet*, p. 3: "La giallezza cagionata dà soverchio amore."

[2] *Memoires*, vol. i., p. 185.

[3] III. *Carnet*, p. 93 and last: "Ogniuno mi dice che li disegni contra me non cesseranno, finche si vedrà che appresso di S. M. vi è un potente partito contro di me, e capace d'acquistar lo spirito di S. M. quando mi succeda una disgrazia."

lar indignation against the author of this plot and those who had shared in it. Now the apparent author of the plot was the Duke de Beaufort, aided by his principal officers together with some gentlemen in the service of the Vendômes. It was necessary, therefore, to arrest Beaufort and to bring him to trial. One may judge from this of the authority which Mazarin had gained, and how far Anne of Austria might one day be induced to go to defend a minister who was so dear to her. Before the death of Louis XIII., the Duke de Beaufort had been the man in whom the queen had most confided, and for some time he had been thought destined to fill the *rôle* of favorite. Since then, he had greatly injured his cause by his presumption and his evident want of ability, and, most of all, by his public intrigue with Madame de Montbazon; but the queen still retained a great weakness for him, and to sign an order for his arrest at the end of three months, was a great step, necessary, it is true, but still extreme, and giving a manifest proof of an entire change in her heart and her intimate relations. Even the dissimulation which she uses in this affair, marks the deliberate firmness of her resolution.

The second day of September is truly memorable in the history of Mazarin, and we may also say in that of France, for it witnessed the consolidation of royalty, shaken by the death of Richelieu and of Louis XIII., and the defeat of the party of the Importants. They did not rise again until the period of the Fronde, five years after, when they reappeared still the same, with the same designs and the same policy, and, after raising fierce and withering storms, were broken anew against the genius of Mazarin and the invincible fidelity of Anne of Austria.

On the morning of the 2d of Sep ember, Paris and the court were filled with commotion at the report of the ambuscade which had been lying in wait for Mazarin the night before between the Louvre and the hôtel de Clèves. The five conspirators who had shared in it with Beaufort, namely, the

Count de Beaupuis, Alexandre and Henri de Campion, Brillet and Lié, had fled and were in safety. Beaufort and Madame de Chevreuse could not follow their example; to fly for them would have been to denounce themselves. The intrepid duchess did not hesitate, therefore, to appear at court as usual; and at the soirée of the 2d of September, she was found at the side of the queen with another person, a very different enemy of Mazarin, a stranger to these dark intrigues and even incapable in her innocence of giving credence to them, the pious and noble Madame de Hautefort. As for the duke, with his usual unconcern and bravery, he went in the morning to the chase, and in the evening, as was his custom, to pay his homage to the queen. When entering the Louvre, he met his mother and his sister, Madame de Vendôme and the Duchess de Nemours, who had been with the queen the whole day and had perceived her agitation. They did all that they could to prevent him from entering, and begged him to conceal himself, at least for a time. Without discomposure, he replied to them as formerly to the Duke de Guise, "They dare not touch me," and entered the presence of the queen, who received him with the best possible grace, and asked him all sorts of questions concerning the chase, "as if," says Madame de Motteville,[1] "she had nothing else on her mind." On the arrival of the cardinal, she rose and told him to follow her. It seemed as if she wished to hold a private council in her chamber. She proceeded thither, followed only by the cardinal. At the same time, the Duke de Beaufort, on attempting to depart, encountered Guitaut, the captain of the guards, who arrested him, and commanded him to follow him in the name of the king and queen. The prince, without seeming at all astonished, gazed at him fixedly, and said, "Yes, I will do so; but this, I confess, is somewhat curious." Then, turning to Madame de Chevreuse and Madame de Hautefort, who were there

[1] Vol. i., p. 185.

conversing together, he said to them, "Ladies, you see that the queen arrests me." "The next morning," continues Madame de Motteville, "while the queen was at her toilette, she did two of her maids and myself the honor to say to us that two or three days before, being at Vincennes, where M. de Chavigny had given her a magnificent collation, she had seen the Duke de Beaufort in a very merry mood, and that a thought of pity had suddenly crossed her mind, and she had said to herself involuntarily, 'Alas! in three days, perhaps, this poor boy will be here again, a prisoner, when he will not laugh.' And Filandre, the first waiting-maid, has assured me that the queen wept that evening on retiring." The good maid of honor, always careful to conceal or to deny all that might injure her mistress, and to point out every thing that may place her in a favorable light, delights here in displaying her gentleness and her humanity. We see above all a profound dissimulation in the conduct of Anne of Austria which even Madame de Motteville cannot fail to remark. It is evident that every thing was concerted in advance between the queen and Mazarin; and if the tears which she shed on this occasion showed how much it cost her to imprison an old friend, they also proved how dear the new friend must have been to have obtained such a sacrifice.

The next morning, the Duke de Beaufort was conducted a prisoner to that same château of Vincennes where he had been but a few days before to promenade and to partake of a collation with the queen. The people of Paris, always friends to bold enterprises when successful, were in nowise excited by the disgrace of him whom they would one day adore; and on seeing the future king of the faubourgs and the market places pass on the road to Vincennes, they applauded, much to Mazarin's satisfaction, and cried with exultation, "Here is the man who tried to disturb our peace."[1] The most dangerous

[1] III. *Carnet*, p. 88: "Tutto il popolo gode e diceva: eccolà quello che voleva turbar il nostro riposo!"

of the Importants received orders to withdraw from Paris. Montrésor, Béthune, Saint-Ybar, Varicarville, and some others, were confined in the country under strict surveillance, or even forced to quit France. The Vendômes were commanded to retire to Anet;[1] and the château d'Anet soon becoming what the hôtel de Vendôme had been in Paris,—the asylum of the conspirators,—Mazarin demanded them of the Duke César, who took good care not to deliver them. The cardinal was compelled almost regularly to besiege the château. He threatened to enter it by force, to seize the accomplices of Beaufort, and no longer to endure the scandal of a prince who braved justice and the laws with impunity; he believed himself in the right, and was about to take energetic measures when the Duke de Vendôme decided to quit France himself, and repaired to Italy to await the fall of Mazarin, as he had formerly awaited that of Richelieu in England.

The arrest of Beaufort, the dispersion of his accomplices, his friends, and his family, was the first, the indispensable measure which Mazarin needed to take to face the most pressing danger. But what would it avail him to strike the arm if the head were permitted to remain,—if Madame de Chevreuse still remained assiduous in her attendance at court, lavishing attentions and homage on the queen, and thus retaining and making the most of the remains of her former favor to sustain and secretly encourage the malcontents, to inspire them with her confidence, and to raise up new conspiracies? She still held in her hand the scarce-broken thread of the plot, and by her side was a man too experienced to suffer himself to be compromised in such intrigues, but quite ready to turn them to his profit, and whom Madame de Chevreuse was

[1] Madame de Motteville, vol. i., p. 190: "Orders were sent to M. and Madame de Vendôme and to M. de Mercoeur to leave Paris instantly. The Duke de Vendôme at first excused himself on the plea of illness, but to hasten his departure and make his journey more convenient, the queen sent him a litter."

studying to show to the queen, to France, and to Europe, as in every way capable of conducting the affairs of State. Mazarin, therefore, did not hesitate; and on the third of September, the same day of the arrest of Beaufort, Châteauneuf was invited to make his adieux to the queen, and then to retire to his government of Touraine.[1] The ex-keeper of the seals of Richelieu found that it was at least something to have been honorably extricated from disgrace and to have regained the high rank which he had formerly occupied in the service of the king, together with the government of a large province. His ambition, it is true, soared much higher, but he postponed its accomplishment, obeyed the orders of the queen, adroitly remained friends with her, and kept on very good terms with her minister while waiting an occasion to supplant him. He waited a long time, but he did not die without having seen again, for a moment at least, the power which an insane love had caused him to lose, and which a faithful and unwearied friendship again restored to him.[2]

Madame de Chevreuse had not the wisdom of Châteauneuf. She did not know how to put a good face on a bad play, or else she was too far pledged to quit the party so soon. La Châtre, who was one of her most intimate friends and who saw her every day, relates[3] that the same evening on which Beaufort was arrested at the Louvre, "her Majesty said to her that she believed her innocent of the designs of the prisoner,

---

[1] III. *Carnet*, p. 40, "Permissione a Chatonof di veder la regina et ordine di andar in Turena." Olivier d'Ormesson, in his Journal, gives this order under date of September 3, 1643.

[2] Châteauneuf had the seals from March, 1650, when Mazarin exiled himself, until April, 1651. He died in 1653, aged sixty-three years. His tomb and that of his family might formerly have been seen in the cathedral of Bruges; nothing now remains but his statue in marble, with that of his father, Claude de l'Aubespine, and his mother, Marie de La Châtre, executed by Philippe de Buister.

[3] *Memoires*, vol. LI. of the Coll. Petitot, p. 244.

but that notwithstanding she deemed it proper that she should quietly retire to Dampierre, and after a brief stay there, should withdraw to Touraine." Madame de Chevreuse was really forced to go to Dampierre, but instead of remaining tranquil there, she moved heaven and earth to save those who were compromised in her behalf. She received Alexandre de Campion at her house,[1] and furnished him with money and every thing necessary to conceal him safely from the pursuit of the cardinal. Fearless for herself and accustomed to dangers, she troubled herself chiefly concerning the fate of her friends, and knowing that several of them were at Anet, she continually communicated with them. She even commenced to knot new intrigues,[2] and found means of forwarding a letter to the queen.[3] Message upon message was addressed to her to hasten her departure.[4] Both Montagu and La Porte were sent to her.[5] She received them haughtily, and delayed under various pretexts. We have seen that on going to meet her, on her return from Brussels, Montagu had offered, in behalf of the queen and of Mazarin, to pay the debts which she had contracted during so many years of exile; she had already received large sums for this purpose, and she would not depart until after the queen had performed all her promises.[6] She

---

[1] *Recueil, etc.*, p. 133: "I could not desire a greater consolation in my misfortunes than the permission which you give me to go to Dampierre; the fear which you express lest I should have been surprised on the road is very flattering, but I shall take such good care of myself that this will not happen to me. I shall not travel by day, and the nights are so dark that I shall not be seen by any one."

[2] IV. *Carnet*, p. 1: "Hebert, mestre d'hotel di Mma. di Cheverosa, tre volte in tre giorni a Aneto dà M. di Vendomo."

[3] IV. *Carnet*, p. 3: "Lettera per altra stada di Cheverosa alla regina."

[4] III. *Carnet*, pp. 81 and 82: "Allontanar Cheverosa che fà mill caballe."

[5] La Châtre, ibid. See also an inedited letter to La Porte, BIBLIOTHEQUE NATIONALE, II., portfolios of Doctor Valant, p. 107.

[6] III. *Carnet*, p. 86: "Mma. di Cheverosa sortita havendo somme con-

quitted the court and Paris trembling, and with grief in her soul, like Hannibal quitting Italy. She felt that the court, Paris, and the heart of the queen, were the true battle-fields, and that to withdraw was to yield the victory to the enemy. Her retreat was a signal of mourning to all the Catholic party, to the friends of peace and of the Spanish alliance, and, on the contrary, of public rejoicing to the friends of the Protestant union. The Count d'Estrade even came to the Louvre in behalf of the Prince of Orange, by whom he was accredited, to thank the regent officially.[1]

Madame de Chevreuse repaired to her estate of Verger, between Tours and Angers. The deep solitude around her rendered the feeling of her defeat still more bitter. She met Montrésor who had also retired to Touraine, and had several interviews with him.[2] She wrote to Paris to the Duke de

---

siderabili di denari contanti. S. M. sa ben li suoi disegni, e che se li da 200 mil lire, come pretende, vi havrà havute 400 mil lire." Journal of Olivier d' Ormesson: "September 19, I heard Monsieur ask at the council if the two hundred thousand livres which had been promised Madame de Chevreuse had been paid her."La Châtre, ibid.: "She persisted in not departing until she had received some money that had been promised her."

[1] Archives of foreign affairs, FRANCE, vol. cv., letter of Gaudin to Servien, October 31, 1643: "M. d'Estrade congratulated her Majesty in behalf of the Prince of Orange on the banishment of Madame de Chevreuse, saying that she had shown the good intention which she had towards the interest of her allies by this action, as since her arrival the said lady had been scheming an advantageous peace, well knowing that the Spaniards would willingly yield all which the French had taken, provided that one thing might be accorded them, namely, the abandonment of the Swedes and the Dutch."

[2] Montrésor, *Memoires*, ibid., p. 355: "The residence of Madame de Chevreuse, at Tours, gave me opportunity to see her at times, and although this was but rarely, I gained more knowledge of her disposition and the temperament of her mind than I had ever possessed in the time when she was more happy and of greater consideration. Her general desertion by all those whom she had obliged and who were bound in friendship and united in interests with her, caused me to feel how little faith

Guise to know if it were true that he disapproved of her conduct, and to try his chivalry.[1] She corresponded with her mother-in-law, Madame de Montbazon, who was banished to Rochefort, and the two exiles incited each other to attempt every means in their power to overthrow their common enemy.[2] Vanquished from within, Madame de Chevreuse placed all her hopes on the side of the foreign powers. She revived the correspondence which she had never ceased to maintain with England, Spain, and the Netherlands. Her principal support, the centre and medium of her intrigues, was Lord Goring, the English ambassador to the Court of France, who, like his master, and especially like his mistress, belonged to the Spanish party.[3] Craft, the English gentleman whom we

---

can be placed in the men of the present century, as is shown by the state in which a person of this rank is found, thus universally forsaken in her disgrace; this increased my desire of rendering my services with greater assiduity and tenderness whenever opportunities might offer. I was not ignorant that the consequences which might follow the visits I had the honor to pay her might injure me and disturb my tranquillity, but the esteem and respect which I had for her person and her interests induced me to run the risk, always observing the precaution that they should not be too frequent, and that there should not be any dissimulation, either on her part, or on mine. The reverses with which her whole life had been agitated were not yet ended."

[1] IV. *Carnet*, p. 14.

[2] Ibid., pp. 48 and 49: "Più animate che mai et in speranza di far qualche cosa contra me con il tempo."

[3] Ibid., pp. 95 and 96: "26 febraio, 1643 (read 1644), l'imbasciator Gorino, lega strellissima con Cheverosa e Vandomo et altri della corte e fuori. Risolutione di unir questa caballa a Spagnuoli, e disfarsi del cardinale. Il suddetto spedisce di continuo a Cheverosa, Vandomo et altri. É stato sempre spagnolissimo, et hora più che mai. Dice che il cardinale una volta à basso, il detto partito trionfarà. Giar (Jars), confidentissimo di Gorino, è sempre in speranza del ritorno di Chatonof, Craft, più bruglione, più spagnolo, et più del partito del suddetto. . . Ha detto mille improperii della regina . . . S. M. faccià scriver una buona lettera al Re e Regina d'Inghiltera dolendosi del procedere de'suoi ministri e di quello scrisse Gorino, etc."

have almost always met in the suite of Madame de Chevreuse, agitated noisily for her, while the Chevalier de Jars intrigued secretly for Châteauneuf. Under the cloak of the English embassy, an extensive correspondence was established between Madame de Chevreuse, Vendôme, Bouillon, and the other malcontents.[1]

When, in the summer of 1644, the Queen of England came to seek an asylum in France, and went to take the waters of Bourbon, Madame de Chevreuse passionately desired to behold again the one who had formerly received her so kindly; and the Queen Henrietta, who, like her mother, Marie de Medicis, and Madame de Chevreuse, was of the Catholic and Spanish party, would have been rejoiced to have poured out her heart into that of so old and so faithful a friend. But she did not think herself justified in yielding to her inclination without the permission of the queen who had accorded her so noble a hospitality. Anne of Austria replied courteously that her sister the queen was free in all her movements, but afterwards caused her to be privately informed through the Chevalier Jars that it was not proper for her to receive the visits of a person at variance with her Majesty.[2] This fresh disgrace, added to so many others, urged the irritation of the duchess to its height. She redoubled her efforts to throw off the yoke that was oppressing her. Mazarin knew and watched all her manœuvres. He caused the arrest of the controller of her household at Paris, and also, a short time after, of her physician while in the same carriage with her daughter.[3] The duchess complains loudly of this proceeding in a letter which

---

[1] Madame de Motteville, vol. i., p. 233, etc.

[2] *Carnet*, p. 105: "S. Maestà puol dire al commendatore di Giar e a madamigella di Fruges che, sebbenne S. M. per civiltà ha detto che per veder o no Mma. di Cheverosa non se ne curava, ad ogni modo la regina della gran Bretagna non dovrebbe admetter la visita d'una persona che per sua mala condotta ha perdute le grazie di S. M."

[3] Archives of foreign affairs, FRANCE, vol. cvii., letter of Gaudin to Servien, May 31; and Montrésor, ibid., p. 356.

she found means to forward to the queen. She asserts that Mademoiselle de Chevreuse was forced from her carriage, "two archers holding a pistol to her throat, and crying unceasingly, 'kill her, kill her, and the women who are with her!'"[1] She did not fail to protest and to appeal from the

---

[1] "Tours, November 20, 1644. MADAME: Although the only happiness which I had hoped in the exile from your presence was that of meriting your remembrance by the continuance of my duties, I have deprived myself of both, since I have known that this forbearance would be to you the more pleasing token of that obedience which I have always endeavored to express to your Majesty, rather in that way which I believed most in conformity with her wishes than in that which would best have satisfied myself. But as your Majesty has assured me that the length of this absence would not diminish the goodness which she has manifested to the whole world in every thing relating to me, I trust, Madame, that, as you have been able to judge of my respect by the time during which I have denied myself the satisfaction of these duties, I may hope that your Majesty will permit me to have recourse to them on occasions important to my repose. I had self-control enough to restrain myself on the first which presented itself in the arrest of my controller, although you cannot doubt, Madame, in the conviction which I have of his innocence, how much I have been pained at feeling that his being my domestic has been the sole presumption of his crime. But I confess to you that what happened four or five days since in the imprisonment of an Italian physician who has been at my house for some time past, affects me so closely that I cannot believe myself so unhappy as to be refused by your Majesty this vent to my just resentment. This was accomplished with violence unheard of in such cases. Having taken an occasion when he was in the carriage with my daughter, she was forced to alight, two archers holding a pistol to her throat and crying unceasingly, 'Kill her, kill her, and the women who are with her!' This proceeding is so extraordinary that as I expect your justice to render me satisfaction in the person of my daughter, I dare promise myself that your goodness will secure me in future from such rèncounters; and although I have sufficient reason to rely on my innocence for safety, I have had such sad experiences of misfortune that your Majesty will not think it strange if I ask it of her with more earnestness, as having ordered me to remain in this place where I am deprived of the sole happiness which I desire in this world, the only consolation which remains to me is to possess security for myself and my household, and to be able

enmity of Mazarin to the justice of Anne of Austria. But the physician who had been arrested and thrown into the Bastille made confessions which gave a clue to some very serious matters; and an officer of the king's guards was despatched to Madame de Chevreuse with an order for her retirement to Angoulême, together with the charge to conduct her there. In Angoulême was a strong château which served as a prison of state, in which her friend Châteauneuf had been confined ten years for her sake. This memory, which was always present to the mind of Madame de Chevreuse, filled her with alarm; she feared that this was the retreat to which they wished to convey her,[1] and, preferring any extremity to a prison, she decided to re-engage in the adventures which she had confronted in 1637, and to take again, for the third time, the road to exile.

But how changed were all the circumstances about her, and how she herself was changed! Her first exile from France in 1626, had been one continuous triumph. Young, beautiful, and everywhere adored, she had quitted Nancy and the Duke of Lorraine, forever submissive to the sway of her charms, to return to Paris to trouble the heart of Richelieu. Her flight to Spain in 1637 had been a severer trial; she had been forced to travel through France in disguise, to brave more than one peril, and to endure many hardships, to find at the end of all this but five long years of impotent agitation. But she

---

to pray to God in peace that he may crown you with as much prosperity as is desired for your Majesty, Madame, by your most humble and most obedient subject, Marie de Rohan."

[1] Montrésor, ibid. This affair (of the imprisonment of her physician) suffered by a man who was her servant, preceded but a few days that which happened to herself. Riquetti, officer of the king's body guard, was sent to Tours to carry her the order to retire to Angoulême, where he was to conduct her. The fear of being detained there and placed in the citadel under a sure guard, made such an impression on her mind that she resolved to expose herself to all other perils which might happen to her, to avoid that of imprisonment, which she believed inevitable if it were not promptly provided against.

was still sustained by youth and by the consciousness of that irresistible beauty which won her servants everywhere, even on thrones. She had confidence too in the friendship of the queen, and she trusted that this friendship would one day reward her for all her devotion. Now age was beginning to make itself felt, and her declining beauty promised her but rare conquests. She knew that, in losing the heart of the queen, she had lost the greatest part of her prestige in France and in Europe. The flight of the Duke de Vendôme, soon followed by that of the Duke de Bouillon, had left the Importants without any considerable chief. She had learned to her cost that Mazarin was quite as adroit and quite as formidable as Richelieu. Victory seemed everywhere in league with him. Turenne, Bouillon's own brother, solicited the honor of serving him, and the Duke d'Enghien gained him battle after battle. She knew that the cardinal held proofs within his hands which could condemn and imprison her during her whole life. But when all abandoned her, this extraordinary woman did not abandon herself. As soon as the officer Riquetti had signified to her the order of which he was the bearer, she took her resolution with her accustomed promptness, and accompanied by her daughter Charlotte, who had come to join her, and who would not quit her, she gained the thickets of the Vendée and the solitudes of Brittany by cross-roads, and asked an asylum of the Marquis de Coetquen, a few leagues from Saint-Malo. The noble and generous Breton accorded the hospitality which he owed to a woman and an unfortunate. She did not abuse it, and after having deposited her jewels in his hands, as formerly in those of La Rochefoucauld,[1] she embarked with her

[1] She afterwards begged the Marquis de Coetquen to remit her jewels to Montrésor, who restored them to a messenger whom she had commissioned to receive them. But Mazarin was informed of every thing; he knew of the correspondence of the duchess; and he attempted to lay hands on the famous jewels, arrested Montrésor, and held him more than a year in prison. See the Memoirs of Montrésor, ibid. Mazarin, so severe towards Montrésor, whom he knew as a dangerous conspirator,

daughter in the depths of winter, at Saint-Malo, in a small vessel which would take her to Dartmouth, in England, whence she intended to pass to Dunkirk and to Flanders. But the ships of war of the Parliament were cruising in those parts; they met and captured the miserable craft, and carried her to the Isle of Wight. There Madame de Chevreuse was recognized; and as she was known as the friend of the queen of England, the Parliamentarians were disposed to treat her harshly and to deliver her to Mazarin. Happily, she found that the governor of the Isle of Wight was the same Count Pembroke whom she had formerly known. She addressed herself to his courtesy,[1] and, thanks to his intervention, though

---

showed indulgence to the Marquis de Coetquen, whose designs had been honorable. In his *Lettres Francaises* preserved in the BIBLIOTHÈQUE MAZARINE, is the following passage, which does him honor, and which Richelieu would not have written. Fol. 376; to M. the Marquis de Coetquen, May 7, 1645: "From what you have taken the trouble to write to me, I acknowledge the information which you give me concerning the entrance of Mme. the Duchess de Chevreuse into one of your houses. Having conversed upon this with the gentleman whom I send back to you, I esteem it superfluous to write here the particulars which I have told him. Relying, therefore, on his parole, I shall content myself with assuring you that I have received with favor the proofs which you give me of your affection for the service of the king in this adventure. I have not failed to represent all that I ought to the queen, *excusing that which has passed by the reasons which you send me*, and by those which the said gentleman has narrated, etc."

[1] Archives of foreign affairs, FRANCE, vol. cvi., p. 162. Letter of Madame de Chevreuse to Count Pembroke, governor of the Isle of Wight, April 29, 1645: "MONSIEUR, The continuation of my misfortunes obliging me to quit France in haste to preserve in a neutral country the liberty which the power of my enemies wished to take from me in my own, the only way by which I found it possible to avoid this disgrace was to embark at Saint-Malo to pass into England and thence into Flanders, in order to reach the country of Liege, where I might justify my innocence in safety if I could obtain a hearing, or at least shelter myself from the persecution to which the hatred and the artifice of the Cardinal Mazarin has subjected me for a year and a half past. Having taken passage with this design in a bark which I found ready to sail for Dartmouth,

with great difficulty, she obtained passports which permitted her to reach Dunkirk, and thence to gain the Spanish Netherlands.[1]

She resided some time at Liege, studying to maintain, and to rivet more closely between Lorraine, Austria, and Spain, an alliance which was the last resource of the Importants and the only foundation of her own credit. But Mazarin had resumed

where I purposed, on arriving, to send for the passports which I should need to go to Dover and thence to embark for Dunkirk, it was captured by two captains of the ships of war which are under the authority of the Parliament, and brought to this Isle of Wight, of which I have learned with much joy that you are governor, assuring myself from your nobleness and your courtesy that you will not refuse the entreaty which I make you that you will demand of the gentlemen of the Parliament a passport to go hence to Dover and thence to embark for Dunkirk, where the unhappy state of my affairs urges me to repair without delay. I hope the favor from the justice of the gentlemen of the Parliament that they will have the goodness not to detain me, as the confidence which I have in their generosity, and the resolution which I have taken of never rendering myself unworthy of receiving its benefits, may justly cause me to hope for the boon which I shall impatiently expect on the return of the bearer, whom I send expressly for this purpose to London with the servant of your lieutenant in this island, from whom you will receive a more particular account of the accidents of my voyage. I abridge them as much as possible, so as not to weary you by too long a letter; and it suffices to show you my need of your aid in my present position in order promptly to receive the passport which I ask of the gentlemen of the Parliament, and to entreat you to believe that I shall never be fully satisfied until I shall have expressed to you by my services that you have obliged a person who will be through her whole life, monsieur, your very humble and very affectionate servant, MARIE DE ROHAN, Duchess de Chevreuse."

[1] Archives of foreign affairs, vol. cix., Gaudin to Servien, May 20, 1645: "Advices from England say that Madame de Chevreuse is still at the Isle of Wight, and that the Parliament will neither give her vessel nor passport to go to Dunkirk, etc." BIBLIOTHÈQUE MAZARINE. *French Letters of Mazarin*, folio 415, July 22, 1645: "One may judge," says Mazarin, "whether we have a great hatred towards Madame de Chevreuse, since, when she was in the power of the English Parliamentarians, they offered to surrender her into our hands, which we did not care for."

all the designs of Richelieu, and, like him, he strove to detach the Duke of Lorraine from his two allies. The duke was then madly enamored with the beautiful Beatrix de Cusance, Princess de Cantecroix. Mazarin endeavored to gain the lady, and he proposed to the ambitious and enterprising Charles IV., to break with Spain, and to enter into Franche-Comté with the aid of France, promising to leave to him all that he should acquire.[1] He succeeded in bringing into his interest the Princess de Phalzbourg, the sister of Charles and the former mistress of Puylaurens, but then very much fallen in favor, who rendered him a secret and faithful account of all that passed about her brother. Mazarin especially demanded to be kept informed of the slightest movements of Madame de Chevreuse; he knew that she corresponded with the Duke de Bouillon, that she held the Imperial General Piccolomini at her disposal through her friend, Madame de Strozzi, and that she still preserved all her influence over the Duke of Lorraine, despite the charms of the beautiful Beatrix. With the aid of the Princess de Phalzbourg, he followed all her movements and disputed step by step the possession of the fickle Charles IV.,—sometimes victorious, but oftener vanquished in this uncertain struggle.[2]

The victory remained with Madame de Chevreuse. Her ascendency over Charles IV., born of love but surviving it, and stronger than all the new amours of this inconstant prince, retained him in the service of Spain, and foiled all the projects of Mazarin. By degrees, she again became the soul of every intrigue plotted against the French Government. She not only combated it from without, but she continually excited new difficulties within. Surrounded by a few ardent and persevering refugees, among whom was the Count de Saint-

---

[1] IV. *Carnet*, pp. 81 and 82; *Carnet*, v. pp. 18, 68, and 115.

[2] Bibliothèque Mazarine, *French Letters of Mazarin* to the Princess de Phalzbourg; especially those of July 22, 1645; of September 30, of the same year; of November 11, of December 2, and 23, etc.

Ybar, one of the most resolute men of the party, she encouraged the remnant of the Importants in France, and stirred up everywhere the fire of sedition. Passionate, yet always mistress of herself, she preserved a smooth brow in the midst of tempests, at the same time displaying an indefatigable activity in surprising the weak sides of the enemy. Availing herself equally of the Catholic and the Protestant parties, sometimes she meditated a revolt in Languedoc or an invasion in Brittany; sometimes, at the least symptom of discontent manifested by any important personage, she labored to detach him from Mazarin and to win him to her cause. In 1647, her piercing eye discerned in the heart of the Congress of Munster some signs of a misunderstanding between the French ambassador, the Duke de Longueville, and the prime minister, which in fact was with difficulty arranged, and to her belongs the mournful honor of having from that time founded too just hopes on the ill-regulated ambition and the variable temper of the Duke d'Enghien, quite recently become Prince de Condé.[1]

Time advanced, the Fronde broke forth; and the ardent duchess rushed again from Brussels in 1649, and brought to her friends the support of Spain and of her experience. She was then nearly fifty years of age. Years and sorrows had tri-

[1] BIBLIOTHÈQUE MAZARINE, *French Letters of Mazarin*, letter of September 28, 1645, to the Abbé de La Rivière, folio 453. But the most important paper of all, which throws much light on all the intrigues of Madame de Chevreuse in 1646 and 1649, and also on the state of public sentiment in France on the eve of the Fronde, is a memoir of a Spanish agent, whom we have already met in the affair of the Count de Soissons, the Abbé de Mercy,—a memoir addressed to the Government of the Netherlands, in which he shows all that Saint-Ybar, and more especially Madame de Chevreuse, might do against Mazarin if they were better sustained. This piece is entitled: "*Memoire sur ce qui s'est négocié et traite au voyage de l'abbé de Mercy en Hollande entre lui, le comte de Saint-Ybar et Madame la Duchesse de Chevreuse.*" The memoir is dated September 27, 1647, and is signed P. Ernest de Mercy. It forms a portion of the official papers of the Spanish Secretary of State which are to be found at Brussels, in the general archives of the kingdom of Belgium.

umphed over her beauty, but she was still graceful, and her keen penetration, her decision, her boldness, and her genius, remained entire.[1] She had found a last friend in the Marquis de Laigues,[2] captain of the guards of the Duke d'Orleans, a man of spirit and of resolution, whom she loved till the end, and with whom after the death of M. de Chevreuse in 1657, she probably united her destiny by one of those *mariages de conscience* then very much in fashion.[3] We cannot be expected to follow her step by step, and to entangle ourselves in the mazes of the Fronde. It suffices to say that she enacted one of the principal *roles* in it. Attached to the heart of the party and to its essential interests, she guided it through every danger with incomparable address and energy. After relying so long upon Spain, she knew how to separate from it at the right time. She preserved a powerful influence over the Duke of Lorraine, and it is not difficult to recognize her hand concealed behind the ambiguous and often hostile movements

---

[1] Retz, who ends by detesting Madame de Chevreuse because she refused to follow him in his last extravagant project, pretends that, in 1649, she no longer possessed even a vestige of beauty. However, she still retained it in 1657, as may be seen from the portrait of Ferdinand Elle, engraved by Balechou, in the series of Odieuvre, in which she is represented as a widow, with a fine, expressive, and aristocratic face.

[2] The Marquis de Laigues, having gone to Brussels in 1649, to treat with Spain in the name of the Frondeurs, found Madame de Chevreuse there and formed an intimacy with her, as Alexandre de Campion had done in 1641. Retz pretends that when Laigues quitted Paris, Montrésor induced him to endeavor to please Madame de Chevreuse, who could do much with the Spanish Government, and to reach her head through her heart. Laigues was young and pleasing in his person; he succeeded, and both became so strongly attached that they never separated. Note the only fact, very uncertain however, since it rests on a single witness, whence Retz draws his admirable conclusion, which does as much honor to his logic as to his delicacy, "that it was not difficult to persuade Madame de Chevreuse to accept a handsome lover."

[3] Memoirs of the younger Brienne, published by M. Barrière, vol ii., chap. xix., p. 178: "The Marquis de Laigues, who was certainly the *mari de conscience* of the duchess."

of Charles IV. She took the principal part in the three great resolutions which express and recapitulate the whole history of the Fronde from the battle of Paris and the peace of Ruel; in 1650, she was of the opinion that they should prefer Mazarin to Condé, and dared to advise them to lay hands on the victor of Rocroy and of Lens; in 1651, a moment of wavering on the part of Mazarin, who nearly lost sight of her in his own intrigues and in a too complicated policy, together with the pressure of a strong personal interest, the well-founded hope of marrying her daughter Charlotte to the Prince de Conti, brought her back to Condé and procured the deliverance of the princes; and in 1652, the manifold errors of Condé restored her forever to the queen and to Mazarin. She did not participate in the folly of Retz—that of thinking a third party possible in the midst of revolution, and dreaming of a government shared between Mazarin and Condé and supported by a worn-out parliament and the fickle Duke d'Orleans. Her political instinct taught her that, after so much agitation, a firm and steady rule was the greatest need of France. Mazarin, who, like Richelieu, had never combated her but with regret, sought and often gladly followed her counsels.[1] She took her place loftily by the side of royalty; she served it, and it served her in its turn. After Mazarin, she spied out Colbert who was not yet in the ministry, and labored for his elevation and the downfall of Fouquet,[2] and the proud but

[1] See in the BIBLIOTHÈQUE NATIONALE, *fonds Gaigniere*, No. 2,799, an inedited collection of the autograph and cypher letters of Mazarin to the Abbé Fouquet, brother of the future superintendent, in which he unceasingly entreats the advice and good offices of Madame de Chevreuse.

[2] Memoirs of the younger Brienne, vol. i., chap. vii., p. 218: "She formed an alliance with the Colberts, and married her grandson to the daughter of a man who would never have thought, ten years before, of making his daughters duchesses. For this, it was necessary to crush poor M. Fouquet, and she sacrificed him without scruple to the ambition of his competitor. I shall presently relate this intrigue with new details.

judicious Marie de Rohan gave her grandson, the Duke de Chevreuse, the friend of Beauvilliers and of Fenelon, to the daughter of a plebeian of genius, the greatest administrator that France ever possessed. She easily obtained all that she

---

Madame de Chevreuse conducted it with ardor; it was the last of her life." Vol. ii., chap. iv., p. 178: "The Duchess de Chevreuse was at Fontainebleu with the Marquis de Laigues concerning this affair, (that of Fouquet.) She had forced the latter to ally himself with M. Colbert, the minister, who was then only controller of the finances. Having preserved sufficient ascendency over the mind of the queen-mother, she caused her to consent to the overthrow of M. Fouquet, although her Majesty had a friendship for him, because he had always willingly paid her dowry, together with some considerable pensions which the king, her son, had bestowed on her after his majority." To support these facts, we find among the papers of Fouquet which were in the famous casket, and which are now preserved in the armory of Baluze at the *Bibliothèque Nationale*, various letters of a secret agent of the superintendent, warning him that Madame de Chevreuse is working against him, and is endeavoring to deprive him of the protection of the queen-mother. This agent, who must have been a nobleman of the court, had indirectly gained the confessor of Anne of Austria, and learned through him of the manœuvres of Madame de Chevreuse. Letter of June 28, 1661: "Madame de Chevreuse continues closely to question this good man, (the confessor,) but this will avail nothing, and you shall be precisely informed of every thing that she shall say to him." Letter of July 21: "I have not been able to learn any thing more particular of Madame de Chevreuse, but the good confessor came here a short time since to see the person of whom I have had the honor to speak to you already. He related to him all that he knew, and told him, among other things, that some time ago Madame de Chevreuse questioned him closely, that she sent Laigues to him several times, and that she talked in a very devout strain to him in order to gain him, but above all, Monseigneur, that she talked against you. I did not hear in what manner, for this good man said that he had related it to M. Pelisson. It will suffice, therefore, for me to warn you that this good cordelier complains a little because you cited him on making an explanation with the queen-mother, saying that you told her that she went to Dampierre among your enemies, who said things against you to her, and when she denied that she had ever been spoken to in this manner, you told her to ask the father-confessor; and that the queen said to him the next day that she could not comprehend

desired both for herself and her family; she attained the height of credit and of consideration, and, like her two illustrious competitors, Madame de Longueville and the Princess Palatine, she ended in profound tranquillity one of the most restless careers of the seventeenth century.

It is said that, towards the close of her days, she too felt the influence of grace, and turned her eyes, wearied with the mobility of earthly things, towards Heaven. She had seen all those whom she loved or hated fall successively around her—Richelieu and Mazarin, Louis XIII. and Anne of Austria, the Queen of England and her daughter, the amiable Henriette, Châteauneuf and the Duke of Lorraine. Her much loved daughter had expired in her arms in the midst of the Fronde. He who had first turned her aside from the path of duty, the handsome and frivolous Holland, had mounted the scaffold of Charles I., and her last lover, the Marquis de Laigues, though much younger than she, had preceded her to the tomb. She perceived that she had given her soul to vanity; and wishing to mortify the feeling that had proved her ruin, the haughty duchess became the humblest of women. She renounced all grandeur; she quitted her magnificent hotel in the Faubourg Saint-Germain, built by Muet, and retired to the country, not

---

how you knew every thing, and that you had spies everywhere." Letter of August 2: "Madame de Chevreuse has been here, and I have been promised information in respect to things which are of the greatest importance to you concerning this affair, the journey to Brittany, (the journey to Brittany and the arrest of Fouquet took place in the beginning of September,) certain secret resolutions of the king, and the measures taken against you." Letter of August 4: "Madame de Chevreuse saw the confessor of the queen-mother twice while she was here. Yet this simpleton conceals this from M. Pelisson, who, on visiting him, asked him if he had seen her, which he denied as he has since said. He has also told things under the seal of strict secrecy which are of the utmost importance. The person who knows them objects to telling them to me because Madame de Chevreuse is concerned in them, and being so closely related to her, she is reluctant to disclose them to me."

to Dampierre, which would have recalled too vividly the brilliant days of the past, but to a modest villa at Gagny near Chelles. There, far from the gaze of the world, she awaited her last hour, and died in obscurity at the age of seventy-nine, in the same year with the Cardinal de Retz and Madame de Longueville. She would have neither funeral solemnities nor funeral oration; she forbade that they should give her any of those titles which she had learned to despise; she wished to be interred obscurely in the little old parish church of Gagny. There, in the southern aisle near the chapel of the Virgin, some faithful but unknown hand has inscribed on a slab of black marble, the following epitaph:[1] "Here lies Marie de Rohan, Duchess de Chevreuse, daughter of Hercule de Rohan, Duke de Montbazon. She espoused, in her first marriage, Charles d'Albert, Duke de Luynes, peer and constable of France; and in her second marriage, Claude de Lorraine, Duke de Chevreuse. Humility having deadened in her heart all the grandeur of the age, she forbade the revival at her death of the least mark of this grandeur, which she wished to end by burying beneath the simplicity of this tomb, having ordered that they should inter her in the parish church of Gagny, where she died at the age of seventy-nine, on the 12th of August, 1679."

---

[1] Abbé Le Beuf, *Histoire du diocèse de Paris*, vol. vi., p. 133, etc. He cites an author of the times, who says: "In this epitaph, she is neither styled Princess nor even Most High and Mighty Lady; nor is her husband styled Most High and Mighty Prince. She died in this parish, at the priory of Saint Fiacre de la Maison Rouge."

THE END.

www.ingramcontent.com/pod-product-compliance
Lightning Source LLC
LaVergne TN
LVHW011229110826
845150LV00006B/1579

9781425515072